How to Attract Birds

Created and designed by
the editorial staff of
ORTHO BOOKS

Writers
John V. Dennis
Michael McKinley

Photographers
Steve and Dave Maslowski

Illustrators
Cyndie Wooley
Wayne Clark

Designer
Gary Hespenheide

D1403775

Ortho Books

Publisher
Robert B. Loperena

Editorial Director
Christine Jordan

Manufacturing Director
Ernie S. Tasaki

Managing Editors
Robert J. Beckstrom
Michael D. Smith
Sally W. Smith

Prepress Supervisor
Linda M. Bouchard

Editorial Assistants
Joni Christiansen
Sally J. French

Acknowledgments

Editorial Coordinator
Cass Dempsey

Consultant
Craig Tufts, Backyard Wildlife Program,
    National Wildlife Federation

Copyeditor
Toni Murray

Proofreader
Barbara Ferenstein

Indexer
Trisha Feuerstein

Special Thanks to
Deborah Cowder
David Van Ness

Separations by
Color Tech Corp.

Lithographed in the U.S.A. by
Banta Company

Additional Photography
Names of photographers are followed by the page
numbers on which their work appears.
R = right, C = center, L = left, T = top, B = bottom.

Susan M. Lammers: 60
Michael Landis: 27, 59T
Michael McKinley: 24
Ortho Library: 61T
Jeffrey Rich: 62
Hugh P. Smith, Jr.: 36L, 44L
Vireo: 45

Front & Back Cover Photography
Steve and Dave Maslowski

Address all inquiries to:

Meredith Corporation
Ortho Books
1716 Locust St.
Des Moines, IA 50309–3023

If you would like more information on other
Ortho products, call 800-225-2883 or visit:
www.ortho.com

3	4	5	6	7
00	01	02	03	04

ISBN 0-89721-452-8
Library of Congress Catalog Card
Number 94-67709

How to Attract Birds

Birds in the Wild

Birds are specialized creatures, with special needs. How they meet those needs in nature shows us how to offer food, water, and shelter in the garden.

Birds are among the most visible and attractive forms of life on earth. Their beauty, song, and power of flight have always fascinated humans. But how many of us know precisely how birds differ from other forms of life and why so many of them have learned to live close to humans and benefit from their presence?

Certain characteristics of birds are obvious. They have feathers. Most birds fly. They lay eggs, and they sing. They belong to the class *Aves* and are grouped into orders, families, and species. Only mammals rank higher in the evolutionary scale than birds. But, unlike birds, mammals have fur, bring forth their young alive, and have teeth. Ornithologists think there are approximately nine thousand species of birds in the world. Approximately eight hundred of these inhabit North America.

Birds are divided into two groups: waterbirds and landbirds. Although many of the waterbirds—including swans, ducks, and geese—respond to food offered to them in city parks, only landbirds come regularly to our yards and accept such benefits as food, water, and housing in the form of birdhouses.

Birds of prey also visit our yards. They are not always after smaller birds. They also prey on such creatures as squirrels, mice, voles, snakes, and grasshoppers. If hungry enough, hawks will take suet and any kind of meat they can find.

The ancestors of birds were reptiles. Birds retain several reptilian characteristics: reproduction through egg laying and body surfaces covered by scales which appear on birds as feathers. Feathers keep birds warm and enable them to fly. Birds go through molting periods—usually in late summer or early fall, and again in spring—during which older feathers are gradually lost and replaced by new ones.

To keep their feathers in tip-top shape, birds must frequently groom and clean them, bathing even during winter. Some species, including

Like all birds this Carolina chickadee needs water, food, shelter, and a nesting site. By providing these you can attract a wide variety of birds.

Seed-eating birds, such as this cardinal, have strong beaks for cracking tough shells.

birds have become specialists and are dependent on a limited range of food and shelter. Some have lost the ability to fly; some, such as the ostriches, have become large, strong runners. Others—the penguins—have specialized in underwater swimming, becoming so proficient they can chase and catch fish.

The birds that visit home landscapes have not become overly specialized. They have remained generalists, able to adapt readily to changes in their environment. They have been quick to take advantage of the benefits humans offer them. Observing their behavior can teach us much about attracting them.

Food

Birds choose their menu from the wide variety of resources that nature provides. Foods they eat include insects, spiders, and worms; nuts and seeds; berries and other soft fruits; flower nectar; tree sap; the tender buds of shrubs and trees; eggs and nestlings taken from other birds' nests; other birds; fish and small animals; and the corpses of small and large animals.

The bill of a bird is a clue to its food preference. The northern cardinal is an example of a group of birds commonly called *seedeaters*. These birds have a strong, cone-shaped bill with an angled cutting edge at the base. Such a bill is well adapted for cracking hard, dry seeds. Other seedeaters include the finches, grosbeaks, towhees, sparrows and juncos, the indigo bunting, and the pine siskin. These birds depend on seeds the year around, although they also eat insects. Their diet contains a greater proportion of bugs in spring and early summer, when seeds are relatively scarce and when the birds' developing young need the concentrated protein that insects provide.

Woodpeckers have strong, pointed, chisel-like bills that are useful for probing and chipping into wood. With its bill the woodpecker can not only excavate deep into trees, searching for preferred insects, but also hollow out cavities for nesting and roosting.

Brown creepers have slender, down-curved, sharply pointed bills for probing into the crevices of tree bark for insects and their larvae. Swallows and flycatchers scoop insects out of the air with wide-gaping bills surrounded by bristles. The bills of American robins and thrushes are poorly adapted for cracking hard seeds and nuts, so they eat mostly insects and

house sparrows and quail, engage in dust bathing, which helps keep the feathers in good shape and may help get rid of small external parasites. Some birds take ants in their bills and anoint their feathers with formic acid, an irritating chemical found in ants. This is called anting and may serve the same functions as dust bathing.

HOW BIRDS MEET THEIR NEEDS

Like all creatures, birds require four basic things to survive: food, water, protection from the elements and danger, and a place to raise their young safely. In nature, birds go about fulfilling these needs in a variety of ways.

Birds have been around a long, long time—at least 140 million years. Over the eons of evolution birds have acquired some traits and lost others to become enormously varied. Some

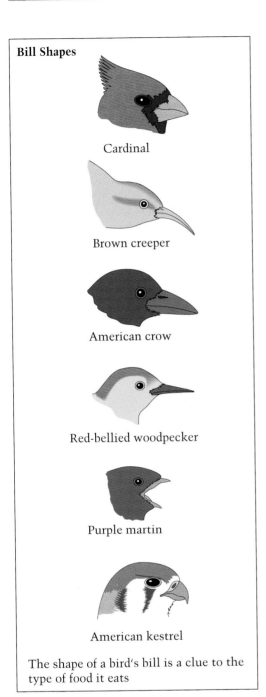

Bill Shapes

Cardinal

Brown creeper

American crow

Red-bellied woodpecker

Purple martin

American kestrel

The shape of a bird's bill is a clue to the type of food it eats

Birds seek out water for drinking and bathing.

soft fruits and berries. American kestrels and shrikes have sharp, curved bills (which, when they belong to birds of prey, are called beaks) that are useful for tearing the flesh of the animals they eat. Some birds, such as American crows, have generalized bills and can eat practically anything.

Of course, the shape of its bill isn't the only physical factor that determines a bird's choice of food. Strong fliers such as swifts and swallows, which feed on the wing, eat almost nothing but flying insects. The owl's hearing is so acute that it can detect the location of a mouse under leaves in total darkness, as well as the direction of its movement. The American robin can actually see the subtle movements of earthworms just below the surface of the soil. Much is still to be discovered about the sensory abilities of birds and how the abilities of different species affect the food preferences of that species.

Water

All birds need to consume water to survive. A few desert birds not ordinarily found in gardens are able to extract all the water they need from hard, dry seeds, but most birds must make frequent trips to a source of open water so they can drink.

In nature birds find their water in rivers, ponds, lakes, and streams, as well as in less obvious sources: raindrops; puddles; dewdrops; snow; and, in some cases, sap, nectar, and moist fruits. In the garden, a birdbath or pool

Cardinals are bold birds that approach water directly.

may attract a greater variety of birds than any food we can provide.

Birds vary in the way they approach water. Some strong fliers, like swifts and swallows, dip into water while on the wing. Open expanses that allow unrestricted flight are most attractive to them. Those species that dwell in mature forests or thickets, such as the wood thrush and rufous-sided towhee, approach water slowly, in a long, cautious process. They prefer water right next to cover. Most garden birds like a water source somewhere between the two extremes, far enough from surrounding vegetation to offer surveillance against a surprise attack, yet close enough for refuge. These birds often approach water by perching in a nearby tree. Then they drop down for a quick drink and a splash, followed by preening on a tree branch. It is not unusual for birds to return for one or two more baths before settling down to dry and preen themselves.

Protective Cover

Sooner or later even the most dedicated flier has to come back to earth, if only to breed. Because birds are so dependent on flight for safety, they are most vulnerable when they are "grounded" to rest, feed, or nest.

To a bird, protection means staying both comfortable and safe. We usually think of a

bird's protection as intimately connected with the kind of plants that it seeks for cover. A scarlet tanager might find protection from the hot sun, the cold wind and rain, or the prying eyes of predators high in the branches of a tree. A northern bobwhite might take cover on the ground under a clump of grass. But protection can take many forms besides the cover of plants. Some birds hide and rest in geological formations, such as a cave used by a cliff swallow or a high rocky ledge that provides a refuge for rock doves.

Plumage is a bird's first defense against an often-hostile environment. The dense covering of feathers that all birds have insulates them from the damp and cold, retains vital body heat, camouflages them from predators, and makes efficient flight possible.

Some birds, such as the male northern cardinal and the male northern oriole, have colorful plumage the year round. The color of a bird's plumage, however, most often reflects the kind of plant cover a bird seeks for protection. The greenish yellow of many warblers is difficult to distinguish from the sun-dappled foliage of the trees they inhabit. The dusky browns of thrushes blend well with the piles of leaves and grasses they frequent under shrubs close to the ground.

The fact that females of nearly all bird species have developed plumage that blends

A covey of bobwhites finds cover in dry winter leaves that disguise as well as protect them.

with their environment shows that camouflage is a distinct advantage to birds. Many male birds, such as the scarlet tanager and the American goldfinch, exchange their bright breeding colors for duller ones in winter.

The kind of protective cover a bird seeks is dictated by a host of factors besides plumage color, however. For example, the type of feet a bird has limits the surfaces it can move and rest on and, hence, its choice of cover. Songbirds, which include about three-fifths of the world's known species, and many garden birds, are referred to by scientists as *perching* birds. This is a more accurate term than *songbirds* because some of the birds in this category don't really sing. They all do, however, have a specialized foot structure in which three toes point forward and one toe points backward to oppose them. This foot structure makes them adept at clinging to cylindrical objects like tree twigs, branches, or grass stems. Nuthatches are perching birds with an even more specialized foot. These birds have long toes and sharp claws that help make them expert climbers, even to the point of being able to climb down a tree trunk head first.

Quail and other ground birds also have three toes pointed forward and one backward, but their feet and legs are strong, with long, clawed toes they use for scratching food from

This fox sparrow has three toes that point forward and one that points backward, making perching easy. The feet of perching birds lock onto a branch; the birds don't have to actively hold on to keep from falling.

the ground. Although fast fliers for short distances, quail are such good runners, walkers, and specialized groundfeeders that they apparently take to the air only when they have to. California quail have been clocked running at 12 miles per hour. It is no accident that their preferred cover is close to the ground in grasses and shrubs.

Chimney swifts have feet with all four clawed toes pointing forward. This configuration enables them to cling to rough vertical surfaces such as the insides of the hollow trees and chimneys in which they roost and nest. But the structure of their feet makes the birds virtually helpless on the ground. Most woodpeckers have four long toes—two pointing forward, two pointing backward, for bracing—which they use for clinging and climbing on rough surfaces such as tree trunks.

A Place to Raise Young

No other bird activities seem to fascinate bird lovers as much as nest building and the raising of young. The artistry and resourcefulness many birds display in nest building are among their most interesting characteristics. The variety of techniques and materials used, and nesting sites chosen, is almost unbelievable. Types of nests range from the rock dove's rough platform of sticks and twigs on a high ledge to the elaborate cup nests of many perching birds, hidden in the crotch of a tree or shrub.

The lucky person who discovers a hummingbird nest realizes how the phrase "work of art" applies in the world of birds. Meticulously constructed of plant down and fine fibers and decorated with moss and lichen, this minuscule nest is nearly impossible to distinguish from a bump on a limb. Some hummingbird species attach nests to the upper surfaces of horizontal limbs. Other hummingbirds attach their nests to vines, hanging ropes, or even light fixtures. Each nest is held firmly to its place of attachment by strands of spiderwebbing.

Woodpeckers dig out nesting holes in tree trunks, often dead or dying ones, by using their strong, pointed bills. Bluebirds, house wrens, chickadees, and all the other birds for which we build birdhouses depend on the cavities made by woodpeckers, and on other natural holes, for nest sites. In some areas modern practices of clean forestry, agriculture, and gardening have seriously reduced the number of hollow or dead trees available to these birds.

Some birds, such as barn swallows, attach their nests with sticky mud to vertical surfaces such as cliff faces or buildings. For these birds the availability of mud is a necessity. Birds that build cup nests in a tree or shrub may also require mud for construction. The American robin begins her nest with pellets of mud, smearing them around with her breast.

Orioles weave pendulous nests, suspended from the delicate tips of branches that seem scarcely able to support their weight. These sacklike structures are stunningly wrought from plant fibers and hair, tightly woven, and lined with plant down and soft feathers.

Left: This tiny nest belongs to a ruby-throated hummingbird. The top edge is lined with spiderwebbing, and the "siding" is lichen. From below, the nest looks like a bump on the branch.
Right: Birds incorporate any suitable material into their nests. This mockingbird is bringing home a length of nylon cord.

Top: Mockingbirds make cup nests. This one is mostly of twigs and stems.
Bottom: Great crested flycatchers are known for their habit of hanging a discarded snake skin from the nest hole, as if to frighten off intruders.

Perhaps the most familiar kind of bird nest is the cup nest tightly interwoven within the crotch of tree limbs or shrub branches. Some, such as the nests of warblers and vireos, display amazing sophistication in their tight, strong weaving patterns and variety of materials. The nest of the American goldfinch is so tightly woven that it will hold water. In fact, if the parents are unable to return to the nest in time to protect the nestlings from rain, the young ones may drown.

Birds that build cup nests usually start with an underlying structure of sticks and twigs, to which they add an astounding array of building materials: grass, leaves, plant down (thistledown is a favorite of goldfinches), strips of bark, silk from the webs of spiders and cocoons of caterpillars, pine needles, mosses, feathers, and animal hair. Some birds, such as titmice and orioles, will line their nests almost entirely with animal hair if given the chance; horse and cattle hair are favorites and may be collected from living animals. Pets as well as wild and domestic animals are common subjects of "hair

This northern oriole has pulled together several twigs to enclose and hide her nest.

nesting materials can be an important criterion for choosing a nesting site.

Convenient sources of food and water are also vital factors in choosing where to raise a brood. For their size, infant birds are exceedingly hungry. They can eat as much as one and a half times their weight each day. Feeding them means many energy-draining trips for parents, so the parents' food demands are also higher than usual. As is the case with many seedeaters that feed insects to their young, the dietary demands of young birds may be different from those of their parents. The availability of food for the nestlings is another important factor in the selection of a nest site.

Parents usually moisten dry foods before feeding them to their infants, so at nesting time the demand for water is often greater then usual. Some parents even carry water to young in their bills—a difficult task over any distance. It's no wonder that many garden birds prefer to nest near a source of drinking water.

From the time an egg is laid until the young bird is able to fend for itself is the most dangerous period of its life. Cold wind and rain are especially hazardous. Predation of eggs and young by other birds and animals takes a heavy toll, too.

For their first broods of the year, birds choose nest sites that are protected from the cold winds and rain of early spring. Later broods are usually raised in a deciduous tree, whose summer foliage offers protection from the sun. A high cliff; a dense, thorny shrub; and an end of a flimsy branch are examples of sites that offer protection from predators. Nests are generally built in the same kind of cover that adults use the rest of the year for protection.

The connection between *how* a bird survives and its habitat, or *where* it lives, is intricate and complex. A bird's specialized behavior and physique may cause it to focus on the resources it is able to use—for example, to exploit a plentiful food source that no other bird can use as efficiently. Availability of food, water, and protective cover are obviously important in determining where a bird lives, but availability consists of two factors: the actual presence of a resource and whether or not a bird is able to use it. If we understand where and under what conditions a bird chooses to live in the wild, we are better equipped to attract that bird to the areas around our homes.

raids," and tufted titmice have been known to pull hair from human heads. Over thirty species of birds attach castoff snake skins to their nests. The skin is either woven into the nest or dangles from it as though a warning sign to keep predators away. Crested flycatchers and blue grosbeaks are known for their habit of using snake skins. When natural materials are scarce, birds can be quite resourceful with man-made stuff. String, yarn, tissue, and strips of plastic are favorites. The availability of

RANGE

The broad geographical area within which all the individuals of a species of bird are found is called the *range* of that species. Years of observation by thousands of people across the country have been compiled to form *range maps* for each bird species found in North America. A range map is given for each bird described in the chart beginning on page 75. The boundaries of a range can be the result of many factors. Birds' movements are limited by physical obstacles, such as mountain ranges or great bodies of water over which they cannot or will not fly. Climate too plays an important role in determining range. For example, the aridity of a desert might prove inhospitable to a particular species; another species might not be able to withstand cold conditions.

A bird's environment is seldom static. Ranges can shift, dwindle, or grow because of broad environmental changes, such as long-term climatic shifts or human alteration of the landscape. Ranges can also change seasonally. On one hand, the needs of a bird frequently change with the season; the specialized needs of nesting and breeding are often quite different from the generalized needs of simply surviving. On the other hand, the habitat itself may undergo dramatic changes as the seasons progress, and these changes affect available food, water, and plant cover. Therefore, a species of bird can have more than one range, depending on the season. These ranges are usually called the *breeding range* and the *wintering range*, although these terms are a bit misleading. Some birds move into their wintering range soon after breeding is over, in late summer. Most birds stay around their breeding range for some time after the young have left the nest. In an area where the breeding and wintering ranges coincide, and where a species of bird may be seen the year around, the bird is known as a *permanent resident.*

Some birds, such as the northern cardinal, are permanent residents in a fairly restricted area, where individuals spend their entire lives, both summer and winter. Other species roam from one place to another as conditions such as climate, food and water, and competition change locally. Only when the movement of a bird is regular and seasonal, however, is it called *migration.* The distance of migration may be short and local, as is the twice-annual

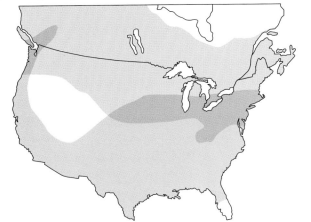

Sample Range Map

This map shows the range of the cedar waxwing. The breeding range is shown in beige, the winter range in blue, and the permanent range in green.

hike of some quail up and down a mountainside. Or it may be dramatically long, like the purple martin's yearly flight to South America. Migration is an interesting specialization developed over thousands of years.

When migratory birds are occupying their summer, or breeding, range, they are called *summer residents*; when in their winter range they are called *winter residents.* When they are traveling in between, in an area not their summer or winter range, they are called *transients.*

Northern cardinals are permanent residents in their range. They live in the same place all year round. Other birds are nomads, moving continually to find advantageous habitats. Still other birds are migratory, flying great distances from summer to winter ranges.

HABITAT

Knowing the range of a particular bird species is just a start to understanding its habitat. The broad area on a map that indicates the range of a species is only a generality, with some concentrations of large populations and other areas in which species may not be found at all. A bird's *habitat* is simply where it lives, including all the elements of its environment—plants, air, water, soil, climate, other birds, and animals. All these elements interact in complex ways to form the unique habitat of a species.

Plants are a most important habitat element. They are a source of food for many birds, yielding fruits, berries, nuts, seeds, greens, sap, and nectar. Living plants and their decomposing remains are the main food of most insects,

Plants are key features in any habitat, and they often determine which bird species will live in the area. Mourning doves prefer solid nest sites, such as the crotch of this tree.

which in turn compose a large part of the diet of some birds. Plants provide nesting sites and comfortable resting spots, protecting birds from unfavorable climate and helping conserve their energy. They also provide a refuge from predators so that birds may venture forth to eat and drink. In some cases they even manufacture moisture by creating sap or nectar or provide access to moisture by collecting rain or dew.

Where Birds Live

Ecologists classify habitats in many different ways, from very broad categories, such as forest or desert, to very specific subdivisions of enormous variety such as the edge of a forest pool or a desert oasis. This chapter will discuss where those birds frequently found around our homes live in nature and relate those natural habitats to the combinations of plants and structures usually found in gardens. Therefore, this chapter will exclude discussions of habitats that are not really useful for attracting birds that live in the home landscape—habitats such as tundra or a saltwater marsh. The following discussion focuses on two broad categories that appear in many variations throughout North America: forest and open country.

As you have read, birds tend to be specialists in their habitats. Because they are such mobile creatures, a few birds that live around human homes depend on a single resource to survive. When they deplete the resources, they move on. Some birds make use of different resources in different seasons. Some find an advantage in exploiting a variety of resources.

Edges, such as this border between trees and a sumac-filled field, attract many bird species. Modern landscaping provides many edges, making our yards attractive to a wealth of birds.

For example, one species might use a meadow rich in insects and the seeds of grasses for food and use a nearby woodland as a nesting site.

The edge between two types of vegetation is the place where the advantages of both are most convenient. As you might expect, these areas tend to support the widest variety of bird species, as well as the greatest number of individual birds.

Edges often occur gradually over distance. A woodland might blend into a grassland over many miles, with trees and shrubs gradually becoming farther apart. Or edges can occur abruptly, as when an isolated grove of trees grows in open country or when thickets adjoin a forest stream.

Abrupt edges can provide certain structural advantages to birds, such as a high spot to watch for danger or prey or a corridor for flight. Abrupt edges may also supply islands of concentrated resources not as available in the region as a whole. The attractiveness of edges to birds is the chief reason so many birds live in gardens, taking advantage of the rich variety of trees, shrubs, flower beds, hedges, lawns, and even buildings.

Birds of the Forest

A bird may inhabit a forest because of the kind of trees it finds there. Some feeder birds, such as pine siskins and purple finches, prefer coniferous forests—the spruce, fir, and pine forests of high altitudes and the North. The western hemlock and redwood forests of the moist Pacific Coast are home to birds such as the varied thrush. Blue jays and red-eyed vireos are found mostly in deciduous forests—the beech-maple forests of the Northeast or the somewhat drier oak-hickory forests of the Midwest. Many garden birds that live in dense forests, however, prefer mixed forests of both evergreen and deciduous trees. Evening grosbeaks, for example, depend on the seeds of both maples and conifers.

A forest, moreover, includes other kinds of plants besides trees. Under the canopy of trees grow a number of layers of understory, including shade-tolerant trees and shrubs and the ground-covering plants that grow in the relative darkness of the forest floor. Birds often favor a particular forest layer. Scarlet tanagers, for example, spend most of their time in high treetops. Wood thrushes, whose large eyes are

well adapted to the gloom, forage under shrubs on the forest floor.

Extent is another quality that defines a forest for many birds. Some shy forest dwellers rarely seen around the home landscape require hundreds of thousands of acres of uninterrupted forest. Some of the garden birds that dwell in forests, however, readily cross spaces between broken forest and scattered trees to inhabit smaller woodlands or relatively open areas in winter. In the chart on page 18, the birds listed as deep-forest dwellers are those most likely to be found in gardens with trees that are close to an extensive woodland.

Forest openings and margins—such as a space where trees have been logged, or a grassy meadow, or a pocket of bedrock or poor soil that doesn't support the demands of trees—are important edge formations in the forest. For many birds these edges provide expanded and varied resources. American robins forage for earthworms in the moist soils of meadows and woodland glens and nest in trees at the edge. Screech-owls tend to hunt over open spaces and nest and roost in trees.

Forest openings are generally characterized by the density and variety of shrubs, small trees, and herbaceous plants that thrive in the sunlight. Especially at the margins of these openings, where the shade-tolerant plants of the deep forest grow vigorously because of

Downy woodpeckers are forest birds that depend on deciduous trees for food and shelter. However, they are comfortable in open areas and are often found around homes if large trees are present.

A brook through a forest offers an unrestricted flight path as well as water and the advantages of an edge habitat. Many birds can be found in a site like this.

hand, the birds can spot ground-moving predators more easily than in dense forest. To minimize the chance of being seen and maximize the chance of seeing, most birds spend their time at the margins of forest openings, making only quick forays into the treeless space.

Because openings contain few trees to restrict flights, they lend themselves well to this dash-and-hide movement. Whether openings are long and linear, like a roadway or utility right-of-way, or closed and circular, birds often use them as flight pathways and corridors to make their way through a broken forest, racing through the exposed spaces to the protection of woodland on the other side. A special group of forest-opening habitats are those created by bodies of water—lakes, ponds, or rivers. Not only does water provide opportunities for drinking and bathing and foster insect life for food, but the moister soil around it encourages a greater abundance and variety of plants. And, like any forest clearing, a body of water among trees offers unrestricted flight space and better surveillance of ground-moving predators.

Woods in a bottomland, the land bordering a river or wide stream, are especially inviting to certain birds. Trees common to the bottomlands of the East include sycamore, elm, ash, tupelo, and maple. These trees, which are tolerant of waterlogged, compacted soils, are commonly planted to line suburban streets. The northern oriole prefers to nest in an American elm, the screech-owl in a hollow sycamore.

Birds of Open Country

A few garden birds almost never leave the cover of brush; they live in thick, uninterrupted shrubbery. The wrentit, a bird of the Pacific Coast brushlands, seldom crosses open spaces of more than a few feet. And a few birds sometimes found in gardens, such as swifts and swallows, which hunt on the wing, prefer open grasslands without obstructions to their flight. But most open-country birds that inhabit the home landscape (see the chart on page 18) prefer mixed brushlands, in which patches of shrubs and small trees are interrupted with patches of grass and wildflowers.

Shrubby open-country habitats vary in the kinds of plants they support and therefore in the variety of birds likely to be found there. Abandoned agricultural fields in the East— with grasses, wildflowers, shrubs, and small

greater light and merge with the sun-loving plants out in the open, the vegetation is dense and varied. Some areas offer expanded resources for birds: a greater variety of fruits and seeds, more insects that feed on the plants, and a wider choice of nesting sites and cover. Where dense forests border open country, you can usually find populations of birds from both habitats.

For forest-dwelling birds, an opening, especially one with low-growing vegetation, can offer increased danger as well as increased safety. In an opening, the birds can be easily spotted, especially by an airborne predator such as the sharp-shinned hawk. On the other trees—provide a variety of heights at which birds can forage and hide, as well as a profusion of rich food-bearing plants. Junipers, hawthorns, wild blackberries, and blueberries provide fruits for birds such as the northern bobwhite, northern mockingbird, and cedar waxwing. Wildflowers such as sunflowers, asters, and goldenrod provide seeds in fall and winter for birds such as the American goldfinch.

The dense evergreen shrubs of the Pacific Coast chaparral, the sagebrush of the western plains, and the mesquite and cactus scrub of the desert Southwest are examples of habitats dominated by shrubs and grasses. These environments lack the water necessary to support trees. A wide variety of birds make their homes in these areas. Some—the California quail and cactus wren—are found only in these habitats. Others—the white-crowned sparrow, northern mockingbird, and house finch—are also found in the moister brushlands of the East.

In shrubby habitats the counterpart to the opening of a forest is the island, or prominence, which may consist of a grove of trees or a single isolated tree. A utility pole or even a fencepost is a sort of prominence that might make very open country inhabitable to some birds. Examples are the red-headed woodpecker, which often nests in such places, or the northern mockingbird, which uses a perch for territorial song.

Many of the birds that frequent forest openings are also found in the islands of refuge provided by groves of trees in open country. Birds that roam use such groves as stopping-off places. Other birds comfortable in open areas use islands for the additional food and cover they provide. Some, such as the red-tailed hawk, require such groves for nesting.

Particularly in the dry shrubby habitats of the West, an island may indicate water. Water flows off the hard surface of a rocky outcrop and concentrates at its periphery, sometimes in enough volume to support vegetation denser than that in the surrounding area, or even a grove of trees. Water may build up seasonally, as it does in a desert wash, and be stored beneath the soil surface. The resulting vegetation may be quite dense.

In open country, the vegetation encouraged by the year-round water of rivers and streams, and the springs and pools of oases, creates dense islands of resources for many birds.

Although birds that use such open-country formations are different from those that use forest waterside openings, the advantages the two areas offer are similar: increased protective cover, greater feeding opportunities, and protected flight corridors.

Many open-country birds seem to prefer waterside thickets, but frequently reside in similar habitats in which water is comparatively scarce. Yellow warblers and song sparrows, for example, can often be found in roadside and fencerow shrubbery, and in the hedges and shrub borders of yards and gardens. In similar ways, many beautiful birds find ways to thrive around our homes and in our gardens.

American goldfinches frequent open fields, where they can find the flower seeds they most enjoy.

Birds That Visit the Garden and Their Preferred Natural Habitats

In this chart and the accompanying text, bird habitats are categorized to provide information that you can use to attract birds to the home landscape. The text parallels the chart in breaking down the natural habitats and relating them to the plant groupings found in gardens. The chart can also be used to predict which birds are most likely to be found in a particular kind of landscape.

Few of the species listed here exhibit a strong preference for only one kind of habitat. Even for those that do, it would be misleading to say that they can't be found elsewhere. The wood thrush, for example, strongly prefers moist woodlands with nearby water, but it can also be found in drier woodlands, and even in relatively open country under dense shrubs.

Some birds use one kind of habitat for breeding and another kind for winter foraging. The yellow-rumped warbler, for example, can be found in many kinds of open-country habitats in winter, but it retreats to dense mixed forest for breeding. Many birds, in fact, are most specific about habitat choice during the stressful

Bird	Open Country			Forest					
	Waterside Vegetation	Isolated Prominence	Mixed brush, Grass	Margin on Open Country	Waterside Vegetation	Broken; Openings	Deep Deciduous	Deep Coniferous	Deep Mixed
American crow		•		•	•				
American goldfinch		•	•	•	•				
American kestrel		•		•					
American robin		•		•	•				
American tree sparrow	•		•	•					
Anna's hummingbird	•				•	•			
Barn swallow	•								
Bell's vireo	•		•	•					
Black-capped chickadee		•				•	•		
Black phoebe	•				•				
Blue jay							•	•	
Brown creeper							•	•	•
Brown thrasher			•	•					
Brown towhee	•		•						
Bushtit		•		•	•				
Cactus wren	•		•						
California quail	•	•	•						
Carolina chickadee		•				•	•		
Carolina wren		•		•		•			
Cedar waxwing	•	•	•	•		•			
Chestnut-backed chickadee					•				•
Chimney swift	•								
Chipping sparrow	•		•						
Cliff swallow	•								
Common grackle		•	•		•	•			
Dark-eyed junco		•	•	•	•	•	•		•
Downy woodpecker					•	•	•		
Eastern bluebird		•		•					
Eastern phoebe					•				
Eastern screech owl									
European starling		•	•						
Evening grosbeak							•		•
Golden-crowned kinglet				•		•			•
Gray catbird	•	•		•					
Hermit thrush						•	•	•	•
House finch		•	•						
House sparrow		•	•						
House wren				•	•	•			
Indigo bunting	•		•	•		•			
Mourning dove	•	•		•					

time of breeding, and more willing to explore different places after the young have flown.

Other birds find similar resources in what, to our eyes, are quite different habitats. The edge of an isolated grove in open country, for instance, is frequently used in much the same way as the edge of a deep forest opening.

A purple finch in a deciduous forest

Bird	Open Country			Forest					
	Waterside Vegetation	Isolated Prominence	Mixed brush, Grass	Margin on Open Country	Waterside Vegetation	Broken; Openings	Deep Deciduous	Deep Coniferous	Deep Mixed
Northern bobwhite		●	●	●					
Northern cardinal	●	●	●	●					
Northern flicker	●	●		●		●			
Northern mockingbird		●		●					
Northern oriole	●	●			●	●			
Orchard oriole	●	●			●				
Pine siskin		●		●		●	●		
Plain titmouse		●		●				●	
Purple finch	●	●			●	●	●		●
Purple martin	●								
Red-bellied woodpecker					●	●			
Red-breasted nuthatch							●		●
Red-eyed vireo		●		●		●		●	
Red-headed woodpecker	●	●		●	●				
Red-winged blackbird	●		●						
Rose-breasted grosbeak		●		●		●			
Ruby-crowned kinglet				●		●	●		
Ruby-throated hummingbird					●	●			
Rufous hummingbird				●	●	●			
Rufous-sided towhee	●		●	●		●			
Scarlet tanager									●
Scrub jay		●	●						
Song sparrow	●	●	●						
Steller's jay							●	●	
Summer tanager					●	●			
Tree swallow	●								
Tufted titmouse		●			●		●	●	
Varied thrush					●		●		
Warbling vireo	●	●							
Western bluebird		●		●		●			
White-breasted nuthatch							●		●
White-crowned sparrow	●		●						
White-eyed vireo	●	●	●	●		●			
White-throated sparrow	●		●			●			
Winter wren					●		●		
Wood thrush					●				
Wrentit	●		●						
Yellow-bellied sapsucker					●	●			
Yellow-rumped warbler		●	●	●		●			
Yellow warbler	●	●		●		●			

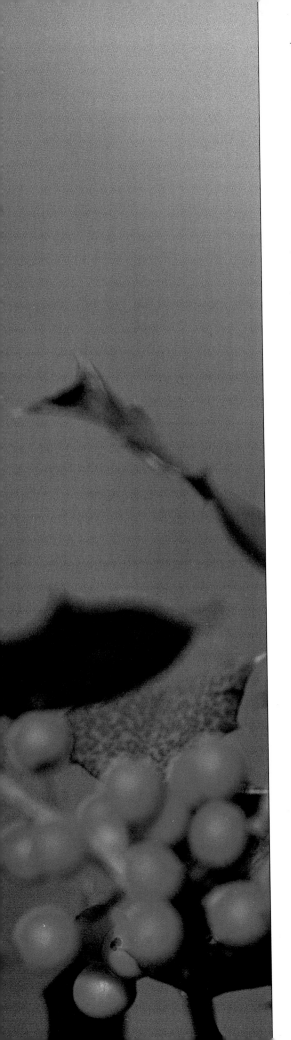

Planting For Birds

Plants are the most important element in the home landscape to birds as well as to you. No matter what size your yard or garden is, no matter whether the style is formal or natural, you can use plants to enhance its attractiveness to birds.

A wide variety of birds love the home landscape. Chances are that your home grounds already suit the tastes of many species, since human ideals of beauty and usefulness in the garden frequently result in concentrations of food, water, and shelter that are particularly appealing to birds.

As horticulturists use selection and propagation to increase the fruit and flower production, growth density, and foliage longevity of native plants, the resources of birds in the home landscape are improved. Because we also use many exotic plants—those native to distant regions—our outdoor areas provide birds with a greater abundance and variety of food and shelter than many of their natural habitats. Even if all you have is a lone pyracantha bush, you are providing birds with an attractive fruit they could not find in the American wild.

The rich soil, water, and fertilizer that we lavish on our home landscapes promote a lushness of growth and abundance of food that birds seldom find in the natural world. Because the space of our yards is limited and because we support them with extra care, food-producing plants are usually more densely concentrated in yards and gardens than in nature.

The home landscape—with its combination of plants, open space, and buildings—offers many parallels to natural habitats for birds. The density, lush good health, and variety of the plants in yards and gardens often resemble that of the waterside growth so attractive to many birds, especially when the open spaces of lawns appear with the vertical, cliff-like surfaces of walls. In the western part of North America, where natural habitats consist largely of grassland and brush, even a lone garden tree can be an important bird refuge. In that dry, sparse country, a garden with only a few plants can perform many of the same functions for birds as a natural oasis or grove. In the eastern part of North America, where natural habitats are dominated by dense forest, an open lawn can

This holly provides berries and shelter for an eastern bluebird.

often be an attractive feature for birds that inhabit forest edges and openings. (These kinds of birds outnumber all others in the home landscape.)

The countryside surrounding your home and the kinds of bird habitats it supports are important in determining the kinds of birds that you will be able to attract to your home grounds. After all, birds are not great respecters of fences and property lines. Because they tend to exploit a variety of resources, nearby areas—a neighbor's pond or grove of trees, a golf course, a wildlife refuge, or agricultural fields—will greatly influence the number and types of birds that can be enticed to your outdoor areas.

Just as birds don't heed human boundaries, neither are they concerned with human concepts of style and beauty. No matter what style of home landscape you have, from the rigidly formal to the wildly naturalistic, your outdoor space can serve the functions of a bird habitat.

Even though your home landscape may already be hospitable to many birds, by intensifying the resources that attract them, you can encourage a wider variety of birds to spend more time there. This chapter will discuss plants as a means of attracting birds—their selection, placement, variety, and relationship to one another. Subsequent chapters will discuss feeding stations, water, and birdhouses and nesting materials.

Even if you have no intention of changing the plants in your yard, you will still find this chapter useful in evaluating why your garden attracts birds, and why they tend to congregate in certain places. Locating and intensifying these nodes of bird activity will help you make your garden more attractive to birds with minimal effort. No matter what style of garden you have, or the stage of development it is in, you can modify it through the selection and placement of plants.

THE ELEMENTS OF THE LANDSCAPE

An ideal bird garden contains elements common to many gardens—trees; shrubs; flower beds; lawn; a house; and the paving of patio, drive, and walk. Perhaps the plants in your garden are not mature, or perhaps you are just beginning to establish a new landscape. Even the youngest landscape can be quite attractive to birds. If your outdoor space is tiny compared to that of an average suburban lot, or even if all you have is a windowsill, deck, or urban courtyard, you can still "borrow" birds from neighbors and nearby habitats. In fact, no individual bird landscape, no matter how ideal, can be considered anything but a part of a much larger bird garden that is at least neighborhood-size. As you plan your bird garden, think in terms of continuity—that is, how to appeal to birds likely to be in the area. Also think in terms of contrast, or how to give them something special that they may have difficulty finding nearby. The contexts of bird gardens in different regions are entirely different. Whatever you have to work with, you can make your garden more attractive to birds.

Ideally, the bird landscape has three main qualities. First, it provides abundantly and in a variety of ways the resources that birds need: food, water, protection from the elements and from danger, and a place to raise young safely. Second, it concentrates these resources in locations that offer the best opportunities for bird-watching, either close to the house and patio or in areas where the observer can hide

A sumac shrub provides abundant food for this tufted titmouse. In spring and summer, the bird browses the leaves for insects. Later, it feeds on the berries.

The Ideal Bird Garden

When it comes to bird gardening, no single "ideal" is applicable to all situations. This plan is presented, not because it might fit your location exactly, but to illustrate some important concepts about what birds find attractive. This ideal garden provides food, cover, and nesting sites in a variety of ways, and it is richly stocked with the plants birds like the most.

This garden capitalizes on the surrounding countryside. To the left are old homes with a lot of mature trees, and a forested park lies beyond them. To the right are new homes with shrubs and lawns, with some abandoned agricultural fields farther away that will eventually be developed into homes. If it were completely surrounded by a forested neighborhood, this garden might be considered a large woodland opening. If it were completely surrounded by open lands, it might be seen as an isolated grove, or an oasis.

This garden capitalizes on birds' fondness for edges. The garden itself lies at the transition between two major habitats and a variety of edge formations are pronounced features. The effect of the "woodland openings" at the upper left is intensified by dense plantings of understory shrubs and small trees and the addition of a small pool. The "oasis" in the back lawn, and the "riverside" of a hedge- and tree-lined street at the front, are also excellent places to incorporate water. The house is surrounded with dense foundation shrubs and vines and a small grove of trees to resemble a "prominence" of lush plants around a rock outcrop. Where one type of vegetation merges into another, such as lawn into the "forest edge" at the upper right, is an excellent spot to concentrate resources like bird feeders. Ideally, these transitional zones should be within easy view of the house.

comfortably. Third, the bird garden includes a variety of vegetation types.

This chapter will discuss three types of home landscapes: shady landscapes composed mostly of trees, which simulate forest habitats; open landscapes planted mostly with shrubs and lawn, which are like open country; and small landscapes. Mixed landscapes containing features of all three may be the most common of all. For suggestions about specific plants as attractors for specific birds, consult the lists beginning on page 29.

If Your Landscape Is Mostly Trees

Your heavy stand of trees gives you an advantage in attracting birds of the forest—it is a feature many homeowners wait a lifetime for. Nuthatches, brown creepers, thrushes, and tanagers are only a few of the special birds that may visit your woodland garden.

As you have read, understory layers, edges, and openings, are very appealing to many birds, and these transitional zones are an important feature of a bird garden. Where mature trees abut the open area of a lawn, gardeners often plant borders of shrubs and flowers. The result resembles the thickets of woodland margins. A pocket of lawn protruding into the shady part of the garden, so that it is partially ringed by trees, resembles a woodland opening. Other low, open areas—the paving of patio and driveway, ground covers or flower beds bordered with trees and shrubs—also function as woodland openings.

Birds frequently use the smooth, flat surfaces of lawn or pavement in some of the same ways they use wet meadows or bodies of water. You can intensify the waterside aspects of these garden elements by placing especially lush plantings of hedges and shrub borders at their margins. Such "watersides" close to trees are likely to attract hummingbirds, phoebes, titmice, and orioles, to name only a few.

The suggestions that follow tell how to intensify the edge effect of watersides, forest openings, and understory layers to make a woodland garden even more attractive to birds.

•Plant a few clusters of shade-loving small trees, shrubs, and ground covers under taller

A landscape edge is as attractive to birds as a forest opening or pond might be. This edge provides open area, "meadow" in the perennial border, and "forest" in the shrubs and trees.

A mixture of deciduous and evergreen trees attracts the widest variety of birds.

trees to provide a number of layers for different kinds of birds.

•Let some of the "forest floor" remain as open soil, or mulch it with leaf litter. These unplanted areas will provide an important resource for ground-foraging forest dwellers, such as thrushes.

•Maintain a woodland that is about half evergreen, half deciduous. You can also adjust the plants in the understory to balance evergreen and deciduous plants.

•Take advantage of the openings already built into your landscape by planting their margins with dense shrubs and hedges especially attractive to birds. Lawns, patios, the street, the drive, and walks are all candidates for this treatment. These are also excellent places to increase the effect of "waterside" habitats.

•If you are especially ambitious and have no real open spots in your garden, consider creating an opening by removing a few trees. If you do decide to remove a dead tree or even a living one, think about leaving a 12- to 15-foot stump with a few 2-foot side branches left on it. The stump can house birds that dwell in tree cavities. However, if the tree you remove suffers from root rot, you'd better cut it clear to the ground; the stump is likely to fall over soon.

If Your Landscape Is Mostly Shrubs and Lawn

Sunny landscapes with areas of lawn broken up by shrubs, flowers, and small fruiting trees are most likely to attract birds of neighboring open country. Such birds include quail, northern mockingbirds, American goldfinches, and song sparrows. The previous chapter mentioned that prominences (groves, oases, and isolated trees) and patches of shrubs mixed with grassy areas form important edges for open-country birds. In many open lawns and gardens, these features are already an important part of the landscape.

A sunny, open expanse of lawn is often interrupted by an oasis of shrubs and flowers. The house itself is a kind of island, or prominence, and in many gardens its functional resemblance to a rock outcrop is increased by dense foundation plantings of trees, shrubs, and vines. Birds that might be drawn to garden islands include the red-bellied woodpecker, northern flicker, black-capped chickadee, and warbling vireo. Shrubby "waterside vegetation," such as a hedge along a drive, may be frequented by yellow warblers, northern cardinals, thrashers, and Carolina wrens, among others.

Top: This "island" in a lawn enhances the yard as a bird habitat and attracts many more birds than an unadorned lawn would. Bottom: Natural tree litter—in this case, dry leaves—provides a food resource for many birds, such as a brown thrasher.

The list that follows suggests things you can do to heighten the effects of prominences, oases, groves, and watersides in your home landscape.

•Start by intensifying the prominence you already have—the house—by planting a few trees close to it. Also plant foundation shrubs and vines if you don't already have them. (For a list of vines that attract birds, see page 31.)

•Be sure to leave spaces, or "clearings," between foundation plants and view windows.

Such clearings are excellent spots to concentrate bird resources. By keeping the spaces clear, you can maintain open sightlines to the yard beyond.

•Away from the house, but within viewing distance, establish a second prominence by planting an isolated, fast-growing tree, such as a honeylocust, pin oak, or red maple. Even more effective, especially right away, would be to plant a small grove of five or seven young trees (odd numbers look best in a grouping). If you already have an isolated tree surrounded by plenty of space, you can make it even more attractive to birds by ringing it with a few younger trees of the same kind, as if they were saplings in a developing grove. (For a list of fast-growing trees to plant in small groves, see page 31.)

•If your garden is densely planted with large, uninterrupted beds of shrubs, consider removing some and replacing them with lawn and a bed of flowers to simulate natural flight paths. Openings in brush and scrub habitats are as important to birds as are openings in woodlands. Rather than solid shrubs, most birds prefer brushy habitats broken up by grassy patches.

•Vary the height, density, and fruiting season of your shrub beds by planting tall shrubs, small fruiting trees, and low ground covers.

•At the garden gate or in a quiet seating area in the yard, create a small arbor planted with vines. A nesting shelf for robins or mourning doves is particularly appropriate at such an intimate site.

•If your landscape is mostly lawn, planting a central island of shrubs and flowers and a small fruiting tree is a quick and easy way to make it more attractive to birds. A birdbath and feeder will intensify its usefulness.

•If you're especially ambitious, planting generous beds of shrubs and flowers will do much to increase the allure of the landscape. Or today you can plant the trees that tomorrow will form a bird garden that is a large woodland grove with a central clearing. The birds will enjoy the shrubby habitat while you wait for the grove to mature.

•When it comes to hedges, birds prefer informality. Leave the foliage unclipped, or prune hedges by using selective branch removal. Restrict pruning to winter, if possible, after any loose fruit has been eaten and before birds begin nesting.

•If you have flower beds, leave as many of the spent flowers as possible, to provide food for birds when the seeds ripen. Plant the perennials and annuals that birds favor, especially those whose seed heads are an asset to the fall and winter garden. Ornamental grasses are excellent choices. For other suggestions, see the list on page 29.

If You Have a Small Outdoor Space

The small lawn or garden can be a haven in an urban neighborhood, a welcome pocket of life to birds in a habitat that, to them, resembles a series of barren rocky canyons. Even the spot of foliage provided by a window box or a hanging fuchsia outside a window can attract the attention of passing birds and keep them coming back if inducements are provided. The variety of wildlife that braves the concrete of our cities is amazing. You're fortunate if you live near a park or greenbelt, but it's not necessary for attracting birds. They will seek you out if you supply food, water, protective cover, and sheltered nesting sites.

A vine-covered arbor offers a nesting site for many different kinds of birds.

Consider the following suggestions for creating a small haven for birds.

•Establish a perimeter of small trees around a patch of lawn. In one corner provide a tiny pool backed by a dense planting of shrubs, small trees, and flowers.

•If you have a deck or a terrace, decorate it with planter boxes of flowers and deciduous and evergreen shrubs. To passing birds this habitat will resemble a ledge on a cliff that has caught a bit of soil, seeds, and water. A small tree in a tub can increase the effect of the mini-oasis. Although the greenery you provide will attract birds' attention, you will have to supply concentrated resources of food and water to make them stop and to keep them returning. Many birdbaths and feeders fit nicely on terraces and are attractive to humans. (For a list of dwarf and compact plants appropriate for a deck or terrace, see page 30.)

•If all you have is a windowsill, flower boxes can provide a green spot to draw the attention of passing birds, and blooms for hummingbirds to feed on. Window-mounted bird feeders, hummingbird feeders, and a pan of water about 12 inches in diameter will welcome birds and keep them coming back for more.

Crop Protection

If you are serious about raising vegetables, fruits, and berries, you'll need to protect your crops. The fact is that birds love most of the same fruits we do, and teaching them to come to your garden is an open invitation to raid your orchard and berry patch.

Bird netting is the most practical and effective way to protect trees and shrubs. These mesh nets can be purchased at most garden centers. Birds often eat the flowers of fruit trees, reducing the eventual fruit yield, so put up the nets as soon as the flowers start to open. Throw the netting directly over the tree. Birds will eat the fruit they can reach through the netting, but fruit inside the tree will be protected. To protect small trees or berries, build a frame

of 2 × 2s around the plants and cover the frame with bird netting.

Protect grapes by enclosing each developing cluster in a paper or cheesecloth bag as soon as the fruit sets. Protect corn in the same way, after the ears are pollinated. Don't use plastic bags; heat and moisture will build up inside them.

Tactics such as hanging shiny objects, like pie plates, to flap in the wind or suspending strips of Mylar tape may work for a while. Or make a framework of stakes on both sides of a row of fruits or vegetables and tie string between them in a crisscross pattern. Birds are discouraged from flying between the strings. To further discourage them,

hang strips of aluminum foil from the strings.

Seed-eating birds, such as sparrows and house finches, find newly planted seeds a tasty snack. Protect your crop by placing plastic netting over the seedbed. Remove the netting soon after the seeds sprout, before the plants get too big. To protect a small seedbed, place a cage of wire mesh over freshly planted seed and leave the cage in place until the plants develop several sets of mature leaves. Cages about 10× 10× 24 inches are self-supporting; reinforce larger ones with heavy wire.

Not all birds are destructive in the garden. Many species feed primarily on insects; in fact, birds are one of nature's most effective ways of controlling pests.

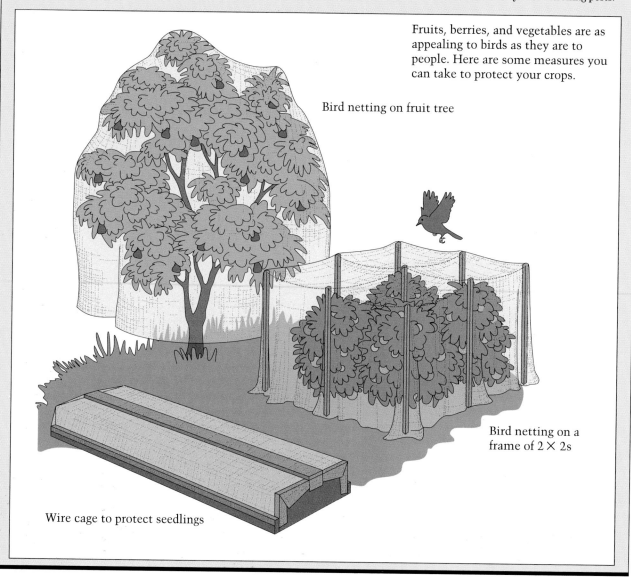

Fruits, berries, and vegetables are as appealing to birds as they are to people. Here are some measures you can take to protect your crops.

Bird netting on fruit tree

Bird netting on a frame of 2 × 2s

Wire cage to protect seedlings

SELECTED PLANTS FOR THE BIRD GARDEN

The plants in the following lists have been chosen for their usefulness and attractiveness to birds and gardeners alike. The Latin name is included in parentheses so you can look up a plant in garden books to get information about growing it. To find out which plants grow best in your area and which varieties will best fill your specific needs, see Ortho's series of gardening books, available at your garden center.

Annuals for Flowers and Seeds

Amaranthus (*Amaranthus,* all species)
Bachelor's-button (*Centaurea cyanus*)
Calendula (*Calendula officinalis*)
California poppy (*Eschscholzia californica*)
China aster (*Callistephus chinensis*)
Coreopsis (*Coreopsis,* all species)
Cosmos (*Cosmos,* all species)
Gloriosa daisy (*Rudbeckia hirta* var. *pulcherrima*)
Love-in-a-mist (*Nigella damascena*)
Marigold (*Tagetes,* all species)
Pinks (*Dianthus,* all species)
Portulaca (*Portulaca grandiflora*)
Sea-lavender (*Limonium,* all species)
Sunflower (*Helianthus,* all species)
Zinnia (*Zinnia,* all species)

Perennials for Flowers and Seeds

Aster (*Aster,* all species)
Butterfly flower (*Asclepias tuberosa*)
Chrysanthemum (*Chrysanthemum,* all species)
Columbine (*Aquilegia,* all species)
Coneflower (*Rudbeckia,* all species)
Coreopsis (*Coreopsis,* all species)
Goldenrod (*Solidago,* all species)
Pinks (*Dianthus,* all species)
Purple coneflower (*Echinacea purpurea*)
Scabiosa (*Scabiosa caucasica*)
Showy stonecrop (*Sedum spectabile*)
Statice (*Limonium latifolium*)
Sunflower (*Helianthus,* all species)

Annual Grasses

Crimson fountaingrass (*Pennisetum setaceum*)
Love grass (*Eragrostis tef*)
Plains bristlegrass (*Setaria macrostachya*)
Quaking grass (*Briza maxima*)

Perennial Grasses

Bulbous oatgrass (*Arrhenatherum elatius* var. *bulbosum*)
Eulalia grass (*Miscanthus sinensis*)
Little bluestem (*Andropogon scoparius*)
Pampasgrass (*Cortaderia selloana*)
Tufted hairgrass (*Deschampsia caespitosa*)

Left: Cardinals, as well as many other birds, are fond of holly berries. Right: Brown-eyed-susans and purple coneflowers, natives of the American Heartland, attract prairie birds.

A cedar waxwing eats mountain ash berries.

Shade-Tolerant Plants for Woodland Understory

Small Trees
American hornbeam (*Carpinus caroliniana*)
Dogwood
  Cornelian dogwood (*Cornus mas*)
  Flowering dogwood (*Cornus florida*)
  Pagoda dogwood (*Cornus alternifolia*) Holly
Holly
  American holly (*Ilex opaca*)
  Nellie Stevens holly (*Ilex* × 'Nellie
    R. Stevens')
Japanese maple (Acer palmatum)
Serviceberry
  Allegheny serviceberry (*Amelanchier laevis*)
  Apple serviceberry (*Amelanchier* ×
    grandiflora)
  Downy serviceberry (*Amelanchier arborea*)

Shrubs
Aromatic sumac (*Rhus aromatica*)
Cherry laurel (*Prunus laurocerasus*)
Dogwood
  Bloodtwig dogwood (*Cornus sanguinea*)
  Gray dogwood (*Cornus racemosa*)
  Redosier dogwood (*Cornus sericea*)
  Silky dogwood (*Cornus amomum*)
  Tartarian dogwood (*Cornus alba*)
Elderberry (*Sambucus,* all species)

Holly
  Chinese holly (*Ilex cornuta*)
  Common winterberry (*Ilex verticillata*)
  Japanese holly (*Ilex crenata*)
  Possumhaw (*Ilex decidua*)
Serviceberry
  Pacific serviceberry (*Amelanchier florida*)
  Running serviceberry (*Amelanchier
    stolonifera*)
Spicebush (*Lindera benzoin*)
Viburnum
  American cranberrybush (*Viburnum
    trilobum*)
  Arrowwood viburnum (*Viburnum dentatum*)
  Blackhaw viburnum (*Viburnum lantana*)
  Hobblebush (*Viburnum alnifolium*)
Yew (*Taxus,* all species)

Plants for Small Places (Good in containers)

Small Trees
Crab apple (*Malus,* all species)
Dogwood
  Cornelian cherry dogwood (*Cornus mas*)
  Flowering dogwood (*Cornus florida*)
Hawthorn (*Crataegus,* all species)
Holly
  American holly (*Ilex opaca*)
  English holly (*Ilex aquifolium*)
  Longstalk holly (*Ilex pedunculosa*)
Hornbeam (*Carpinus,* all species)
Maple
  Amur maple (*Acer palmatum*)
Serviceberry
Allegheny serviceberry (*Amelanchier laevis*)
  Apple serviceberry (*Amelanchier* ×
    grandiflora)
  Downy serviceberry (*Amelanchier arborea*)

Shrubs
Boxwood (*Buxus,* all species)
Firethorn (*Pyracantha,* all species)
Holly
  Chinese holly (*Ilex cornuta*)
  Common winterberry (*Ilex verticillata*)
  Japanese holly (*Ilex crenata*)
  Possumhaw (*Ilex decidua*)
  Yaupon (*Ilex vomitoria* 'Nana')
Honeysuckle
  European fly honeysuckle (*Lonicera* ×
    xylosteoides 'Clavey's Dwarf' and
    'Emerald Mound')

Juniper (*Juniperus*, all species)
Mugo pine (*Pinus mugo* 'Compacta')
Myrtle (*Myrtus communis*)
Serviceberry
  Pacific serviceberry (*Amelanchier florida*)
  Running serviceberry (*Amelanchier stolonifera*)
Shrub bushclover (*Lespedeza bicolor*)
Vernal witchhazel (*Hamamelis vernalis*)
Viburnum
  American cranberrybush (*Viburnum trilobum* 'Compacta')
  European cranberrybush (*Viburnum opulus* 'Compactum')
Yew (*Taxus*, all species, dwarf cultivars)

Fruiting Small Trees and Large Shrubs for Full Sun

Bayberry (*Myrica pensylvanica*)
Beautyberry (*Callicarpa*, all species)
Black mulberry (*Morus nigra* 'Black Beauty')
Blackberry and raspberry (*Rubus*, all species)
Blueberry (*Vaccinium*, all species)
Carolina cherry laurel (*Prunus caroliniana* 'Bright 'n Tight')
Cherry and plum (*Prunus*, all species)
Cotoneaster (*Cotoneaster*, all species)
Crab apple (*Malus*, all species)
Currant (*Ribes*, all species)
Dogwood
  Cornelian cherry dogwood (*Cornus mas*)
  Flowering dogwood (*Cornus florida*)
  Kousa dogwood (*Cornus kousa*)
  Redosier dogwood (*Cornus sericea*)
Elderberry (*Sambucus*, all species)
Firethorn (*Pyracantha*, all species)
Hawthorn (*Crataegus*, all species)
Holly
  American holly (*Ilex opaca*)
  Chinese holly (*Ilex cornuta*)
  Common winterberry (*Ilex verticillata*)
  English holly (*Ilex aquifolium*)
  Longstalk holly (*Ilex pedunculosa*)
  Possumhaw (*Ilex decidua*)
Mountain ash (*Sorbus*, all species)
Pin cherry (*Prunus pensylvanica*)
Rose (*Rosa*, all species especially old-fashioned shrub types)
Sapphireberry (*Symplocos paniculata*)
Serviceberry (*Amelanchier*, all species)
Spicebush (*Lindera benzoin*)
Sumac (*Rhus*, all species)

Western sandcherry (*Prunus besseyi*)
Winter honeysuckle (*Lonicera fragrantissima*)
Viburnum
  American cranberrybush (*Viburnum trilobum*)
  Arrowwood viburnum (*Viburnum dentatum*)

Fast-Growing Trees for Small Groves

Alder (*Alnus*, all species)
Birch (*Betula*, all species)
Eastern white pine (*Pinus strobus*)
Green ash (*Fraxinus pensylvanica*)
Hackberry (*Celtis*, all species)
Oak
  Pin oak (*Quercus palustris*)
  Willow oak (*Quercus phellos*)
Poplar, aspen (*Populus*, all species)
Red maple (*Acer rubrum*)
Staghorn sumac (*Rhus typhina*)
Sweet gum (*Liquidambar styraciflua*)
Tulip tree (*Liriodendron tulipifera*)

Vines (Attaches to rough surfaces without a trellis)

Bittersweet
  American bittersweet (*Celastrus scandens*)
English ivy (*Hedera helix*)
Fiveleaf akebia (*Akebia quinata*)
Grape (*Vitis*, all species and cultivars)
Honeysuckle
  Everblooming honeysuckle (*Lonicera* × *heckrottii*)
  Trumpet honeysuckle (*Lonicera sempervirens*)
Virginia creeper (*Parthenocissus quinquefolia*)

Shrubs for Hedges

Box honeysuckle (*Lonicera nitida*)
Boxwood (*Buxus*, all species)
Cherry laurel (*Prunus laurocerasus*)
Firethorn (*Pyracantha*, all species)
Holly
  Chinese holly (*Ilex cornuta*)
  Japanese holly (*Ilex crenata*)
  Yaupon (*Ilex vomitoria*)
Japanese barberry (*Berberis thunbergii*)
Myrtle (*Myrtus communis*)
Silverberry (*Elaeagnus pungens*)
Yew (*Taxus*, all species)

Hummingbirds in the Garden

Their shining, jewel-like colors and unique habits make hummingbirds among the most fascinating birds you can attract to your home landscape. Their iridescent plumage comes in every hue—fiery red, glowing ruby, deep violet, metallic greens and blues, shimmering bronze, gold, and yellow—the colors changing with the bird's every movement and each shift of the light.

Everything about these tiny birds is interesting. With over 320 different species reported, they are one of the largest bird families. Most species are concentrated in equatorial South America; only 16 species breed north of the Mexican border, and most of those are not widespread. Three of the most common species in the United States—the Anna's, ruby-throated, and rufous hummingbirds—are described in the chart beginning on page 75. The plumage of all three of these species is basically green; even the gorget (throat area) of the male ruby-throat appears green or black in the shade.

Despite their minute size, hummingbirds are extremely strong fliers. The rufous hummingbird is only about 3½ inches long and it weighs only ⅑ ounce, yet it breeds as far north as southern Alaska and winters in Mexico—a migration of over 2000 miles. This migration takes place over several weeks, or even months, as the birds follow the blooming season of their favorite flowers. The ruby-throated hummingbird is even smaller (about 3¼ inches and ⅒ ounce) than the rufous hummer, but it migrates from as far north as southern Canada to as far south as Panama. Its route may cross the Gulf of Mexico—a nonstop flight of 500 miles. In preparation for its long trek, the hummingbird stores up fat, increasing its body weight by as much as 50 percent.

Even when it's not migrating, the hummingbird needs to eat relatively huge quantities of food to fuel its rapid metabolism. In fact, ounce for ounce, hummingbirds require more calories than any other warm-blooded animal (except possibly for shrews). The calories are necessary both to maintain their body temperature of about 105° F, and to fuel their extremely rapid movement. In forward flight, a hummingbird may beat its wings 75 times per second—no wonder we perceive the creature as a blur.

In flight, hummingbirds are uniquely adapted to gathering nectar from their favorite flowers. Not only can they hover motionless before a flower, they can dart backward, up, down, and in any direction so quickly that they seem to vanish from sight. Many species of hummingbird cannot walk at all. To shift positions on a branch or adjust their bodies on the nest, they will simply rise in the air an inch or two, alighting again in a new position.

Feeding

Hummingbirds have two major sources of food: flower nectar and small insects, including spiders. The tiny birds also frequently visit the holes that sapsuckers make in trees, both to drink the sweet sap and to snap up the insects that are also drawn by the sap. Although hummingbirds visit nectar-bearing flowers of all colors, they are most drawn to bright red, pink, and orange tubular flowers. The most important thing you can do to attract these birds to your garden is to plant flowering annuals, perennials, shrubs, and trees.

These birds will come eagerly to special feeders stocked with sugar water. The advantage of feeders is that they bring the birds where you want them—close to the house or other places where they can be easily observed. Several models of hummingbird feeders are available. Bright red plastic flowers will guide the birds on their initial visits, although they will soon learn to seek out their rich food even if the location or appearance of the feeder is changed.

A ruby-throated hummingbird feeds at a trumpetcreeper blossom.

The lichen-covered nest of a female ruby-throated hummingbird.

The formula for hummingbird food is simple: about 1 part white granulated sugar to 4 parts water. Boil the water, add the sugar, stir until it dissolves thoroughly, and let the solution cool. Store unused solution in the refrigerator.

Fill the feeders daily. Every four or five days, take them down and rinse thoroughly with hot water to which a little vinegar has been added; this will prevent mold from becoming established. Scrub the feeders with a baby-bottle brush, and rinse thoroughly before refilling them.

Don't use honey solution in the feeders; it is a likely medium for the growth of a fungus that can infect the tongues of hummingbirds. And don't add red food coloring to the sugar solution, although the color is attractive. Instead, wrap the feeder with red plastic, ribbon, or tape.

The sweet, sticky sugar-water solution is also attractive to insects—including ants, flies, bees, and wasps. If ants find their way to the feeder, apply a generous smear of vegetable oil or petroleum jelly on the wire from which the feeder hangs. This should prevent the ants from reaching the food. To discourage flying insects, try putting petroleum jelly around the feeder openings.

A temporary means of insect control is spraying the feeder with a fine mist from a hose or sprinkler. Insects are discouraged by the water, any sugar solution that has been dropped on the outside of the feeder is washed away, and hummingbirds love to flit in and out of the spray.

Many birds besides hummingbirds are attracted to these feeders—including some sparrows, chickadees, finches, nuthatches, orioles, and downy woodpeckers. If you want to offer sugar solution to birds other than hummingbirds, set up some feeders with perches for the birds that eat while perching. In this way, you can reserve the perchless feeders for the hummingbirds, which usually feed while hovering.

Nesting

The nests of hummingbirds are so tiny—about the diameter of a half dollar—and so well camouflaged that they are seldom noticed. In most cases the male's responsibility ends when the eggs are fertilized. The female constructs her nest primarily of plant down bound with spiderwebs and saliva. The outside of the nest is camouflaged with bits of moss and lichen, so that it is virtually indistinguishable from the branch to which it is attached. Each egg—there are usually two of them—is the size of a small bean. The mother incubates the eggs, without help from the male, for 15 to 19 days, depending on the species.

Newly hatched hummingbirds are almost completely featherless and remarkably ugly, but they are hardier than their size would indicate. The mother feeds them for about 25 days, by which time they leave the nest and begin to fend for themselves. Most hummingbirds raise two broods each breeding season.

Planting for Hummingbirds

Not only do flowers provide nectar, they also attract the tiny insects (especially spiders) that are an important part of the hummingbird's diet. In the wild these birds prefer meadows, lowland forest edges, and woodland openings, especially near running water. To maximize the effect of plantings in your garden, plant flowers in clusters rather than scattering them about. Plant trumpet vines or honeysuckle on a trellis at the back of the garden, with groups of tall-growing flowers in front of it. Plant progressively shorter plants as you work toward the front of the beds, so that your view will be unobstructed. An island of flowers or shrubbery in an expanse of lawn is also welcoming to hummingbirds. Even a window box or container plant with a mass of blooms is likely to attract a tiny guest.

A broad-tailed hummingbird at a desert trumpet.

A broad-tailed hummingbird at Indian paintbrush.

Providing Food

The secret to successful bird-feeding is providing the kind of food each bird prefers and presenting it in ways that make it easy for birds to find and eat it.

Planting for birds and feeding them bring far more birds to our home landscapes than would be the case without these overtures. But it is the feeding stations that bring the greatest number and provide the drama. A survey by the United States Department of the Interior reported that approximately 82 million people in the United States actively participate in feeding wild birds. Some three million people feed birds in Canada. These numbers provide testimony to the rewards of the activity. The only outdoor hobby of this kind that is more popular is gardening. People of all ages are fascinated by watching birds at feeders. For those who are housebound, the hobby has great appeal. The interest of many professional naturalists was first sparked by this first-hand opportunity to see how the natural world works. For birds, feeders are a reliable food source that can be counted on regardless of the weather.

Many people begin feeding birds as soon as cool weather sets in during the fall. This is when winter residents such as juncos begin appearing in yards and when we ourselves are making preparations for the winter. But do birds really need extra food at this time of the year? Probably not. Natural food is still abundant and easily obtainable. Birds are likely to experience shortages only later, after the natural supply has become depleted or inaccessible because of snow and ice.

The most crucial time for birds can be early spring. A snowstorm or blizzard in late March or April can kill birds that have been present all winter and new arrivals from the tropics. Yet the first warm days of spring are a signal for some people to close down their feeding operations. To be on the safe side, continue feeding birds until well after there is any danger of a return to winter weather.

A flock of American goldfinches snacks at a cluster of bird feeders.

YEAR-ROUND FEEDING

If the motive for feeding birds is largely to derive satisfaction and entertainment, conduct a year-round feeding program. The warm months bring a different clientele to the feeder as migratory summer residents return from their southern ranges and winter visitors depart for their breeding places farther north.

Birds tend to scatter at nesting time, becoming more territorial and less social, but the presence of a convenient food source can induce some to nest nearby. Instead of a dozen northern cardinals, only one or two breeding pairs may gather at the feeder. Along with other summer residents—such as resident chickadees, titmice, finches, nuthatches, and woodpeckers—the cardinals will provide a new source of interest. You can now watch the nesting cycle from beginning to end. The cycle includes courtship; nest building; egg laying, incubating, and hatching; and the fledglings' leaving of the nest. In many cases, the parents bring their offspring to the feeders. Following the example of a parent, the young birds learn to gather their own food. But even after they have mastered this art, they continue to demand morsels, crouching before a parent, with wings quivering and mouths gaping. The parent, which may already be busy with a second brood, cannot resist putting something edible into the mouth of the clamoring youngster.

Left: House sparrow fledglings, like many baby birds, demand food by crouching with mouths open and wings spread. The parents, much like human parents, often succumb to begging and feed their offspring.
Right: A young bird fancier and a Carolina chickadee eye each other through a window. Window feeders bring birds close in for clear viewing.

In addition to providing the panorama of the nesting season, summer offers the opportunity to feed hummingbirds. Hummingbirds will visit sugar-water feeders into fall in most parts of the country. In warm areas, several hummingbird species are year-round visitors. For hummingbirds that haven't migrated farther southward, it would be a hardship not to have the artificial nectar that replaces flower nectar as winter sets in.

Many people discover that attendance at bird feeders is at its lowest ebb in early autumn. This is largely because fruits, berries, and seeds are so plentiful at this time of year. Insects and other small invertebrates are also numerous. Nevertheless, chickadees and other permanent residents usually continue daily visits to the feeder, advertising the availability of food for whatever birds come along.

BIRD FOODS

The mainstays of any bird-feeding program are seeds and grains, nutmeats, and fats in the form of suet and suet mixes. Add bakery products, fruit, and sugar water to the list, and there will be foods to meet the tastes and needs of many visitors.

One frequently overlooked "food" is grit. Birds have no teeth, and depend upon hard particles (grit) in their gizzards to grind up whatever passes into their digestive systems.

Grit is especially welcome in areas where snow covers the natural supply. Available in garden centers and feed stores, one common type of grit is composed of ground oyster shell. Seashore sand containing fine particles of quartz is another type. Crushed eggshell is a form of grit that supplies birds with calcium. It is the one food offering that purple martins will accept. Place the shell on the ground below martin colonies during the birds' nesting season. In other cases, place grit in small containers away from bird feeders to prevent it from being contaminated by bird droppings.

Seeds and Grains

Many excellent birdseed mixtures for wild birds are available at garden centers, nurseries, feed stores, and grocery stores, as well as through mail-order bird clubs and outlets. Some commercial mixtures, however, contain a substantial amount of inexpensive seed that the birds at your feeder are likely to ignore. You may find it more satisfying to offer only one type of seed, or to make your own mixture from bulk seed. This allows you to tailor what you offer to attract the birds you want to attract and discourage those you do not want to attract.

The best way to formulate your own mixture is by using a testing tray (see the photograph at right). Such a tray is easy to make. It is composed of a number of separate compartments, one for each kind of seed you offer. Label each compartment with the kind of seed it contains, place the tray at your feeding station, and keep a careful record at the end of each day of the amount of each type eaten. Two or three weeks of testing will give you an idea of the relative proportions for a seed mixture that is tailored to the preferences of the birds in your area. Because preferences and bird populations change, you may want to continue testing throughout the feeding season.

Sunflower seed Almost synonymous with bird feeding, sunflower seed has always been used for feeding cage and wild birds. A black, oil-rich sunflower seed produced especially for bird feeding was introduced around 1980 and is now the most popular seed or grain used in bird feeding. A survey by Project FeederWatch (see page 92) established this fact as well as the reasons for the popularity of the seed, which is called black oil sunflower. Compared

to traditional sunflower seeds, the black oil seed has more meat and less hull per seed and is easier for birds to open. Moreover, the black oil seed, with its high oil content, is richer in protein, fats, vitamins, and minerals. Among those who feed birds, the black sunflower seed is two to three times as popular as the striped sunflower seed.

For those who do not want to be bothered with sunflower hulls that accumulate below feeders, there is an easy solution: Buy shelled sunflower seed. Although more expensive and with a shorter shelf life than unshelled seed, seed meats are quickly eaten by birds and leave no debris.

Jays and squirrels often bury sunflower seeds for later use. As the forgotten seeds

Top: A mourning dove patronizes a grit feeder. In areas without plentiful natural grit, or in winter, grit is a welcome and helpful "food." Purple martins, like many birds that spurn typical offerings, will come to a grit feeder. Bottom: A food-testing tray shows what the birds in your neighborhood prefer. Food preferences vary with the season. Check your tray throughout the year to see how feeding habits change.

When You Can't Be There

And what about the midwinter vacation trip? Won't birds that have been coming to the feeder be hard-pressed while you are gone?

The work of two researchers, Brittingham and Temple, can relieve your worry. Working with wintering black-capped chickadees in Wisconsin, Brittingham and Temple used leg bands to identify individual birds and chart their survival. The researchers found that, during a severe winter, 69 percent of the birds that went to feeders lived through the winter, whereas only 37 percent of those without feeders survived. During a normal winter, there was no difference in survival rates.

Among other findings in the Wisconsin study were that chickadees in winter obtain less than 25 percent of their food from feeders and that shutting down a feeder during a mild winter had no harmful effects on the patrons.

So, you can feel safe in closing down operations for a while during a mild winter. If neighbors are feeding birds, you have no reason to worry even during a severe winter. If you wish, make some long-lasting food like suet available. Or you can ask a neighbor to keep your feeder filled.

Wild birds readily adapt to changes in the food supply. When one food source runs out, they soon find another. You can take that winter vacation and not worry about the birds you have left behind.

---

sprout, they may become troublesome weeds in your garden. Using hulled seeds prevents this problem.

Among birds, sunflower seed is primarily a food for woodpeckers, titmice, chickadees, nuthatches, jays, grosbeaks, cardinals, and other seedeaters. Most such birds, with the exception of the northern cardinal, prefer to have their food served in elevated feeders. Cardinals will eat at elevated feeders if they have an adequate place to perch. Providing sunflower seed on raised platforms or the ground is wasteful because squirrels and other ground feeders will quickly devour it. Offer sunflower seed at hopper and tube feeders shielded from squirrels.

Sunflower seed can be offered the year around. It keeps well, but like other seed having a high oil content, has a tendency to become rancid in hot weather. Also, a grain moth (*Sitotroga cerealella*) may infest seed kept too long in storage. Store sunflower seed, as well as other types of seed and grain, in a container with a tight lid and keep it in as cool and dry a place as possible. For lengths of time that various seed can be safely stored, see the chart on page 50.

Safflower seed   Like sunflower seed, safflower seed is an oil-rich seed used primarily for cooking oil. A native of India, safflower is now being grown in drier parts of the West. Only recently has its virtue as a bird food been discovered: The tough-coated seeds are not eaten by many unwelcome guests but are eaten by birds that most people like. The preferred birds—the seedeaters as well as the omnivorous chickadees, titmice, and nuthatches—are able to crack open the hard seed coats with their bills. Mourning doves solve the problem by swallowing the seeds whole. But the unpopular birds—the European starlings, common grackles, brown-headed cowbirds, and red-winged blackbirds—with their differently shaped bills, are unable to crack open the seeds and do not swallow them. They try for a while but soon give up. Squirrels, a problem species of another kind, are unpredictable in their reaction to safflower seed. Sometimes they eat it, sometimes they don't.

When safflower seed is first offered at a feeder, birds are usually slow to accept it. But if mixed with sunflower seed, they soon catch on. Northern cardinals are one of the first birds to recognize safflower seed as a food. The seeds are pure white and should be offered in tube or hopper type feeders. Seeds that fall to the ground are readily consumed by cardinals and mourning doves.

Store safflower seed in the same way as sunflower seed. If anything, the safflower seeds, with their hard coatings, keep better. They can be used safely the year around, and are regarded by many as one of the best seeds to use in summer. Safflower seed is now available at almost all garden centers and other stores that sell food for wild birds. Thanks to its selective quality, it is becoming more and more popular with those who feed birds.

Niger seed   Also known as thistle seed, niger seed is not the seed from the weed known as thistle. Niger (*Guizotia abyssinica*) is grown in India and Ethiopia for use as cooking oil and in soap. A small black seed, it has long been used as a food for cage birds. In 1972, niger seed, along with a feeder for holding it, was offered commercially for feeding wild birds. Presently, up to 60 percent of Project Feeder-Watch participants in the Northeast and South-Central regions offer niger seed at their feeders. The popularity of this oil-rich seed lies in its attractiveness to small finches that are

able to eat at the special feeders designed to hold it. American goldfinches, pine siskins, common redpolls, purple finches, and house finches are so eager for the seed that they will desert other foods to eat it. However, house finches, when competing with goldfinches, tend to favor black oil sunflower seed if it is also offered.

Another way to get around competition from house finches is to offer niger seed in a feeder that appeared on the market in 1992. Called an anti-house finch feeder, the perches of this feeding station are above the feeding vents instead of below them. Users must hang by their feet in an inverted position to reach the openings! This may sound like a hardship, but it really isn't. Goldfinches, as well as pine siskins and common redpolls, often hang upside down to reach food in the wild. House finches are unable to perform this feat.

Niger seed that falls to the ground is readily consumed by mourning doves, dark-eyed juncos, native sparrows, and other finches. The small seeds are usually scorned by blackbirds

Top: A sampling of birdseeds. Clockwise from the top left, these are safflower, milo, striped sunflower, niger, cracked corn, millet, a finch mix, and black oil sunflower.
Bottom: A perch above the hole in a feeder offering niger means the station is built to favor goldfinches. House finches are unable to hang upside down to feed at it, but goldfinches perform this feat easily.

and squirrels. Chickadees and titmice eat them but prefer sunflower seeds.

Compared to other standard foods used in bird-feeding, the price of niger seed is high. However, a small amount of seed goes a long way. The seeds are eaten by only a select clientele and they are so small that they cannot be consumed very rapidly. It is wasteful to use niger seeds in what are called thistle bags or stockings. Close to half the seed held in the woven mesh bags falls to the ground when birds are eating at them.

Niger seed spoils readily when exposed to moisture. If it remains uneaten for several days, it has probably spoiled and the birds are refusing it. If this is the case, empty the feeder, clean it, and refill with fresh seed.

Corn   Available in many forms, corn can be offered on the cob; as whole kernels; cracked corn, cornmeal, and grits; and in products such as cornbread and mush. Like sunflower seed, corn has long been a standard bird food. Quail, pheasants, doves, pigeons, starlings, cardinals, blackbirds, and house sparrows like various grades of cracked corn. Recipes using cornmeal and other corn products (see page 41) are popular with nearly all birds that come to feeders. Although a universal bird food, corn in its various forms has a few drawbacks. It invites rodents and other undesirable species and, unless blended in a suet mixture to keep it

dry, is subject to spoilage in damp weather. (The whole kernels are less subject to spoilage than cracked corn.) Since corn is a "heating" food, low in protein and high in carbohydrate, use it primarily for winter bird feeding.

Corn is inexpensive and liked by squirrels, making it an ideal squirrel food. Cobs of corn on spikes or hanging from a branch are often used to feed squirrels.

Mixed birdseed   From the standpoint of popularity, only black oil sunflower seed and suet can compete with mixed birdseed. Nearly all ground-feeding birds find something in mixed birdseed and, for those who feed birds, it is easy to use. Standard mixtures consist of millet, milo, wheat, cracked corn, and canary seed, with a few black oil sunflower seeds thrown in. Expensive gourmet mixtures may contain such added ingredients as almond and sunflower meats and niger seed.

Inexpensive mixes often consist largely of inexpensive ingredients that birds do not eat. Milo (a form of sorghum) is particularly prone to being wasted. But this is not universally true. In the Southwest, where it is widely grown, milo is popular with most birds.

Birds, as shown by tests conducted by Dr. A. D. Geis, prefer black oil sunflower seed to other sunflower seed and white proso to other millet. The same tests show that compared to other seeds and grain, birds do not favor

These corncobs are impaled on spikes driven into the tree trunk. Corn is an inexpensive food that can be used to lure squirrels away from expensive birdseed.

This simple ground feeder is pressed into snow. Cardinals, house finches, and a mourning dove enjoy the mixed seed in it.

buckwheat, flax seed, milo, oats, wheat, rice, and rapeseed. But this doesn't mean that you should give up on other ingredients. Birds vary in their tastes. You may discover from tests of your own that the birds at your feeder can't get enough of the so-called unpopular items.

The best way to formulate your own bird-food mixture is by using a testing tray, as explained on page 37. The recipe on this page offers a seed mixture that is useful in most areas. The chart on page 49 gives the food preferences of the most common seed-eating birds.

Primarily a food for ground-feeding birds, offer mixed birdseed on the ground or on open trays or platforms near ground level. Here it will be visible and easily taken by ground feeders. Project FeederWatch has found that mixed birdseed is the first choice of no fewer than 21 species of birds that do most of their feeding on or near the ground. If offered at higher levels, where titmice and chickadees feed, mixed seed has far fewer takers.

Nutmeats   What has been said about corn applies equally well to nutmeats. Peanuts and tree nuts are best offered in winter. This is when birds most need the extra protein and calories in these highly nutritious foods. Like corn, nutmeats are subject to spoiling under hot, humid conditions.

Recommended Birdseed Mix

Many birdseed mixes are available commercially. If you decide to make your own mix, this simple recipe should appeal to many seed-eating birds.

Sunflower seeds (unhulled oil type) 50%
Millet (white proso) 35%
Cracked corn (fine or medium) 15%

Birds seem to enjoy exotic nutmeats as readily as they do native nuts. The almond, a native of Asia and grown in California, is one of the best nuts for bird-feeding. The meats are available at many wild-bird centers.

If you give the birds a little help, they will readily accept nutmeats in the shell. Don't let those hickory nuts, black walnuts, and pecans go to waste. Break the shells open with a hammer and let the birds pick out the meats. However, this practice entails work on your part; you will have to do the pounding and clean up the broken shells.

One of the best feeders for nutmeats, including shelled peanuts, is made of wire mesh. Hang a nutmeat-filled feeder from a horizontal

Top: Woodpeckers and other suet eaters, such as this tufted titmouse, can easily hang upside down to get suet from the feeder. The feeder is starlingproof because starlings cannot hang like this to feed. Bottom: A tufted titmouse tugs a nut from a nut feeder.

line that has been squirrelproofed. Feeders made of $\frac{1}{4}$-inch wire mesh are available at wild-bird centers. The fun begins when chickadees, titmice, nuthatches, and even Carolina wrens cling to the feeders and tug at the nutmeats inside. To prevent the nutmeats from spoiling, bring nutmeat feeders inside when it looks like rain.

Birds are fond of peanuts, whether raw, roasted, or lightly salted. When offered in the shell, they are carried away by jays, who bury them or pound them open and eat the contents. Peanuts are not a recommended offering in summertime, however. Peanut hearts—the embryos of the peanut, which are removed in making peanut butter—are the only peanut product that birds are reluctant to eat.

Suet and Suet Mixtures

Among people who feed birds, the popularity of suet, along with that of mixed birdseed, is second only to the popularity of black oil sunflower seed. Suet is used somewhat more in the North than the South.

Beef suet is the best type to offer birds, and you can purchase it at low cost from a butcher. Be sure to ask for short suet, or kidney suet, rather than stringy suet. Make sure that it is fresh, firm, and white. If you intend to melt it down, ask the butcher to grind it for you. Or you can grind it yourself with a kitchen grinder.

Fill the lower container of a double boiler with water. Place the ground suet in the top container and let the water boil. Heat the suet until it has been rendered to a liquid state. Allow hot suet to cool and thicken before adding other ingredients. Raisins, peanut butter, refined corn products, and a wide variety of fruits are among the bird treats you can stir into the thickening suet before pouring it into forms or packing it into bird feeders. (See the suet recipes at right.)

Ground suet can be purified by heating it, as described previously, allowing it to cool and solidify, and then removing the fat that has risen to the surface. After the fat drains, you can store it in the refrigerator or immediately reheat it and make it into suet cakes. Compared to unpurified suet, purified suet makes harder cakes that last much longer outdoors. Using purified suet is essential when offering suet in the spring and summer. In very hot weather, offer suet in the shade only. If melting occurs, bring the holder and suet cake indoors and refrigerate them. Follow the same procedure at night in any season if nocturnal mammals are a problem. If starlings are a problem, use any one of several starling-proof suet feeders now on the market.

Commercial suet cakes are widely available, and most have the advantage of being highly refined and very hard, characteristics that retard spoilage. Also, storebought suet cakes fit neatly into commercial suet feeders. Many birds prefer the softer homemade mixtures, however, and the special treats you add to them.

Placing seeds in suet mixtures (a common practice) is inadvisable. Mixed birdseeds are for ground-feeding birds and only get in the way when added to suet cakes.

Baked Goods

Birds have a special fondness for baked goods. They prefer white bread over other breads, so it is one of the best foods to use to get birds to come to a new feeder. Offer the bread in the form of crumbs on a platform feeder. This food, like most baked goods, should be exposed for only a few days at the most; otherwise, it will become a moldy health hazard. Other baked goods that have special appeal include pie crust, pancakes, cornbread, cake and cracker crumbs, and doughnuts.

Unfortunately, baked goods sometimes bring unwanted guests to the bird feeder. House

---

Suet Recipes for Insect-Eating Birds

No-Melt Peanut Butter Suet
1 cup lard (no substitutes)
1 cup crunchy peanut butter
2 cups "quick cook" oats
2 cups cornmeal
1 cup white flour
⅓ cup sugar

In a large saucepan melt lard and peanut butter, then stir in remaining ingredients. Pour this mixture into square freezer containers to form a suet layer about 1½ inches thick. Store in the freezer. The suet cakes will not melt in typical summer or warm winter weather.

Soft Peanut Butter Mix
Relished by a wide variety of birds, this mix is great for packing into feeders or smearing on pine cones or tree trunks.

1 cup freshly ground suet
1 cup peanut butter
3 cups yellow cornmeal
½ cup enriched white or whole wheat flour

In a large saucepan melt suet; then add peanut butter, stirring until melted and well blended. In a medium bowl, mix together cornmeal and flour. After the suet mixture has cooled and started to thicken, add the dry mixture; blend. After cooling, the concoction is ready to serve.

Hard Peanut Butter Mix
This mixture will last longer in the out-of-doors than will the soft mixture especially in warm weather.

2 cups suet
1 cup peanut butter
2 cups yellow cornmeal
2 cups fine cracked corn

In a large saucepan, melt the suet. Allow it to cool thoroughly, then reheat it. Add peanut butter, stirring until melted and well blended. Add cornmeal and cracked corn; blend well. Pour the mixture into forms or suet feeders. Let it cool until hardened.

Cornbread for Birds
6 cups yellow cornmeal
3 teaspoons baking powder
⅔ cup shortening
3 pints water

Preheat oven to 425° F. In a large deep pan, mix all ingredients. Bake for 25 minutes. Serve cornbread on a platform feeder or in a suet basket. (From *A Complete Guide to Bird Feeding* by John Dennis)

A Sweet Treat
6 cups water
1 cup shortening or melted suet
2 cups cornmeal
½ cup flour
1 cup white or brown sugar
Raisins, nutmeats, peanut butter (optional).

In a large saucepan, boil the water and shortening. Mix in cornmeal, flour, and sugar. Stir well and bring mixture to a boil. Turn off heat and cover. If you like, add raisins, nutmeats, or peanut butter. Pour mixture into pans. Let it cool, then cut it to size. Store treats in the refrigerator until ready to use. (From *A Complete Guide to Bird Feeding* by John Dennis)

Filler for Suet Feeders
3 cups melted suet
1 cup cornmeal
1 cup peanut butter
1 cup nutmeats
1 cup coarse brown sugar
1 cup raisins or currants

Combine ingredients in the top of a double boiler and add enough water to achieve the consistency of porridge. Cook over hot water until blended. Use to fill coconut shell feeders and other hanging feeders. This is a rich mixture that is well-liked by birds in winter. (From *A Complete Guide to Bird Feeding* by John Dennis)

Left: A hanging dough-nut can attract birds that don't normally come to feeders. This white-throated spar-row, however, is a fre-quent feeder visitor. Right: Fresh fruit at-tracts northern orioles as well as some other hard-to-attract birds.

sparrows, starlings, dogs, and cats are quick to spot baked goods that are out in the open and not in protected feeders. Doughnuts, however, allow you to get around this difficulty. Suspend each doughnut on a wire holder made from a coat hanger that has been straightened except for the hook at the end. Doughnuts can be left out longer than other baked goods, and they may attract such unusual visitors as bluebirds, kinglets, warblers, and orioles.

Fruit

Like bakery products, fruit can be used to bring additional birds to the feeder. This is es-pecially true in the summer, when fruit-eating birds from the tropics appear. But winter is also a good time to offer fruit if late orioles, catbirds, or robins are in the vicinity. There is nothing like a halved orange impaled on a twig or nail (or offered at a feeder designed to hold oranges) to lure an oriole. In freezing weather you may have to replenish the supply at fre-quent intervals.

Oriole feeders made of wood and complete with perches, a roof, and a place to impale halved oranges (or halved apples) are available at wild-bird supply centers. Another way to make fruit available is in a fruit bowl. Simply fill it with berries or cut-up fruit or melon and place it on a feeding shelf or platform. Discard uneaten fruit promptly or it will attract flies.

Raisins and dried currants attract, among others, northern mockingbirds, and cedar and Bohemian waxwings—just about the hardest birds to attract. For best results, steam or soak the raisins or currants in water. Offer the fruit in shallow containers. Once waxwings discover the food, they gorge themselves and keep com-ing back for more. Sliced apple is another food that they will respond to.

As the chart on page 49 shows, fruit can also attract the varied thrush (a West Coast spec-ies); any of the orioles; summer tanagers; and the yellow-breasted chat. The only fruit eater you may have qualms about attracting is the European starling.

Sugar Water

Sugar water is the only food that is recom-mended for feeding hummingbirds. See page 33 for instructions about making and offering a sugar-water solution.

To the delight of some and dismay of others, the specialized feeders that hummingbirds use are also exploitable by many other birds. The orioles, represented by five species, are the most common nonhummingbird guests. Others include titmice and chickadees (6 species); jays (3 species); warblers (13 species); tan-agers (3 species); rose-breasted and black-headed grosbeaks; and the northern cardinal, purple finch, house finch, and American

Orioles are so fond of sugar water that feeders are available with perches spaced just for them.

Predation

Birdwatchers often feel responsible if a hawk or a cat kills a bird in their yards or gardens. They wonder whether their bird-feeding brought numbers of birds to one place where they were unusually vulnerable to predators. Probably not. Studies have shown that the number of birds killed in the vicinity of feeders is actually lower than the number killed in the wild. This may be because birds at feeders obtain their food in a relatively short time; they can devote more time to watching for predators.

Predation is a natural part of birds' lives. A high reproductive rate helps make up for losses from predation, accidents, disease, and weather. Normally, the heaviest losses occur at the nest during the fledgling stage. The young birds' inexperience and poor flying make them easy prey. Birds that survive this period have a fair chance of living much longer. Bird-banding records show that the life expectancy of adult northern cardinals is anywhere from 4 to 13 years. Many of the same birds that spend the winter or summer in your yard come back year after year.

Predators usually take the slow, less-fit individuals. Predation keeps birds alert and prevents them from becoming too sluggish for their own good. Some predation helps keep the species strong and fit.

The advantages of predation notwithstanding, seeing a bird you have come to love be eaten by a hawk or killed by a cat is distressing. You can help protect your guests from predators.

Cats

Although not all cats kill birds, many of them do. The list that follows presents steps to take with your own cat and steps you can suggest your neighbors take with theirs.

•Keep cats indoors as much as possible—especially at night and during the nesting season.

•Place a bell on every cat's collar.

•Use hanging bird feeders and place them at levels no closer to the ground than 4 feet.

•Place birdbaths near trees but not close to dense cover where a cat might hide.

•Call on the services of a yappy dog to keep cats out of your yard.

•Work in your community for the passage of cat neutering and licensing laws.

Hawks

Due to the diminishing natural habitat, hawks are seen near feeders more frequently today than in the past. If a hawk begins visiting your yard regularly, provide cover for the birds. Place shrubs and brush piles near places where birds come to feed, drink, or bathe. Unfortunately, this contradicts one of the steps associated with coping with cats. Choosing which predator to "favor" can be difficult.

goldfinch. Altogether, 68 bird species, other than hummingbirds, have been observed at sugar-water feeders. Following the example of hummingbirds, some have learned to hover briefly at feeding ports and take a quick drink; others use perches or cling to the feeder itself. To make the feat easier for orioles, the same manufacturers that make hummingbird feeders have produced oriole feeders with properly spaced perches.

Sugar water is little more than a taste treat and a quick source of energy; it is not a substitute for other foods.

FOOD PRESENTATION

How food is presented is nearly as important as the type of food offered. Fortunately, the human goal of having birds where we can see them usually coincides with avian preferences; most birds like having their food in the open. Some prefer to feed on or near the ground, others higher up. For this reason, present food at different elevations. To prevent crowding, provide as many feeders as the size of the outdoor space and your inclinations allow. Some should be in windows or close to them, place others well away from windows (for information on avoiding window strikes, see page 53). Place plantings near feeders so birds will have shelter from attack by predators.

Birds are much more visible at some feeders than others. In proofing feeders against the weather and inroads by squirrels and other undesirable visitors, designers have been forced to make feeders that are less open. Some models are so closed that humans have trouble seeing the birds and the birds have trouble reaching the food. Look at several different models before deciding which one to purchase. Feeders should be attractive, long-lasting, weatherproof, and open enough for you to see the birds eating at them.

Of course, presenting food to birds does not have to involve a bird feeder. You can offer food on a roof, balcony, patio, or deck, or on a natural object such as a rock or a hollow in a log. As you have seen, suet mixtures can be smeared into crevices in the bark of tree trunks.

Some Ground and Platform Feeders

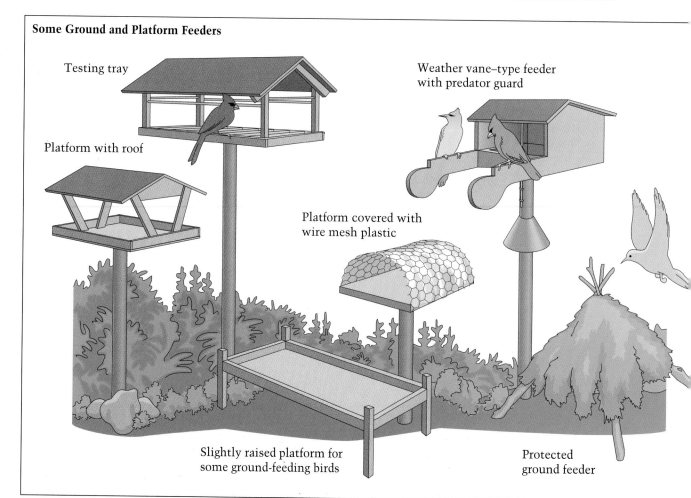

Testing tray

Weather vane–type feeder with predator guard

Platform with roof

Platform covered with wire mesh plastic

Slightly raised platform for some ground-feeding birds

Protected ground feeder

Hopper Feeders

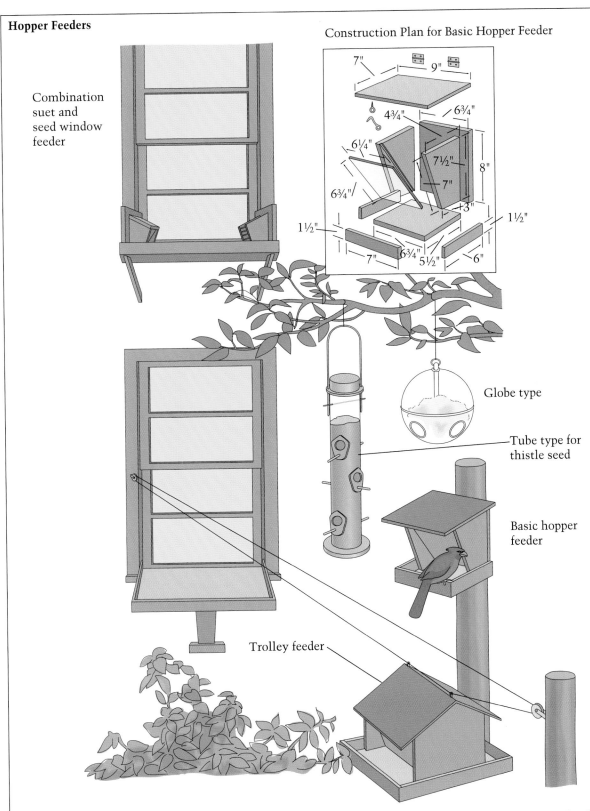

Combination suet and seed window feeder

Construction Plan for Basic Hopper Feeder

7"
9"
6¾"
4¾"
6¼"
7½"
8"
7"
6¾"
3"
1½"
1½"
7"
6¾"
5½"
6"

Globe type

Tube type for thistle seed

Basic hopper feeder

Trolley feeder

To coax birds to a window feeder, start by attaching a feeding tray to a ground floor windowsill. Keep the shades down until the birds become accustomed to the feeder. Keep the windowsill feeder well stocked with fresh food, even though it may be little used at first. Construct a rope-and-pulley apparatus between the window and some object about 15 or 20 feet away, such as a tree or clothespole, from which you will suspend a second well-stocked feeder. Starting with this feeder at its farthest point, move it a few inches closer to the window every day. As it approaches the window, after a few weeks, begin to decrease the supply of food on it, and increase the supply of special treats on your window feeder. Before long you will be able to dispense with the trolley feeder.

Types of Suet Feeders

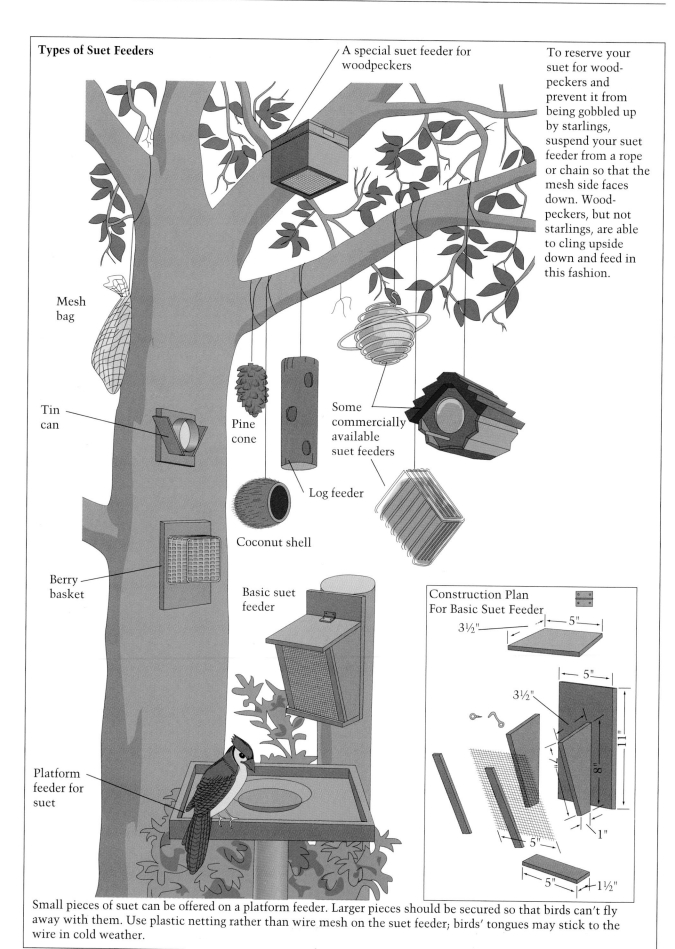

A special suet feeder for woodpeckers

To reserve your suet for woodpeckers and prevent it from being gobbled up by starlings, suspend your suet feeder from a rope or chain so that the mesh side faces down. Woodpeckers, but not starlings, are able to cling upside down and feed in this fashion.

Mesh bag

Tin can

Pine cone

Some commercially available suet feeders

Log feeder

Coconut shell

Berry basket

Basic suet feeder

Platform feeder for suet

Construction Plan For Basic Suet Feeder

3½"   5"

5"

3½"

11"

8"

1"

5"

5"   1½"

Small pieces of suet can be offered on a platform feeder. Larger pieces should be secured so that birds can't fly away with them. Use plastic netting rather than wire mesh on the suet feeder; birds' tongues may stick to the wire in cold weather.

Bird-Feeder Placement

The best way to determine where birds prefer to have their dinner in your yard is by experimenting. Remember, though, that birds are creatures of habit and don't respond well to abrupt changes in the position of feeders.

To attract the most birds, offer a wide variety of feeding spots and types of feeders. For example, different birds like to feed at different heights. A well-rounded bird-feeding program includes several feeding stations, a platform feeder on a post about 5 feet off the ground, a few hopper or tube feeders (for seeds) 5 to 8 feet above the ground, a thistle feeder, a window feeder, and some suet feeders mounted on tree trunks at various heights.

Birds appreciate a variety of surrounding vegetation, also. If you have the space, establish two or three feeding areas about 50 feet apart, each with a variety of feeders at different heights. This allows you to cater to the preferences of different bird species by taking advantage of the different types of plant groupings in your landscape. The groupings may contain open space, a "forest edge" next to a lawn, or a dense woodland. Offering several feeding areas also solves many problems of unruly behavior; the irritable individual that chases other birds off will be unable to defend several feeding areas at once. Flocks of aggressive birds, like starlings, can be diverted with inexpensive foods such as bread crumbs, dogfood, and table scraps placed at areas distant from the house.

Make use of natural "platform feeders" you already have on your property. These include tree stumps, flat rocks, and the tops of walls and fenceposts.

Especially in winter, birds favor the most sheltered locations. Besides being uncomfortable for birds, strong winds can disturb hanging feeders and scatter the food. The south side of the house is generally the warmest; the areas buffered by trees and shrubs offer relatively mild microclimates. Find these sheltered areas in your yard and be sure to use them as feeding areas.

THE PURCHASE AND STORAGE OF BIRD FOOD

The three types of bird food most often purchased are seeds, grains, and nutmeats. Suet and suet cakes can either be purchased or created at home, from recipes. Where to buy these

Favorite Foods of Feeder Birds and Levels at Which They Feed

If a food has not been checked after the name of a bird, don't assume that the bird never eats that food. Knowledge about food preferences is far from complete. Most birds accept food at different levels but generally prefer to eat at ground or near-ground level or at an elevated site.

Bird	Safflower	Sunflower	Niger	Corn	Mixed Seed*	Nutmeats	Suet & Mixes	Bakery Goods	Fruit	Sugar Water	Raised Feeders	Ground Feeders
American goldfinch	•	•	•		•	•	•			•	•	
American robin						•	•	•	•	•	•	
American tree sparrow		•		•	•	•	•	•				•
Black-capped chickadee	•	•	•			•	•			•	•	
Black-headed grosbeak		•		•	•		•	•	•	•	•	
Blue jay	•	•		•	•	•	•	•	•	•		•
California (brown) towhee		•		•	•		•			•		
Carolina wren		•			•	•	•	•	•		•	
Cedar waxwing									•	•	•	
Common grackle		•		•	•	•	•	•		•		•
Common redpoll		•	•		•		•	•				•
Dark-eyed junco		•	•	•	•	•	•	•		•		•
Downy woodpecker	•	•		•	•	•	•	•		•	•	
Evening grosbeak	•	•			•	•	•			•	•	
Gray catbird					•	•	•	•	•	•	•	•
Hooded oriole						•		•		•	•	
House finch		•	•		•	•	•	•	•	•	•	
House sparrow		•		•	•			•				•
Mourning dove	•	•	•	•	•	•	•					•
Northern cardinal	•	•		•	•	•	•	•	•	•		•
Northern flicker					•		•	•	•	•	•	
Northern mockingbird						•	•	•	•	•	•	
Northern oriole					•	•	•	•	•	•	•	
Pine siskin		•	•	•	•	•	•			•	•	
Purple finch	•	•	•	•	•	•	•			•	•	
Red-bellied woodpecker	•	•		•	•	•	•		•	•	•	
Red-breasted nuthatch	•	•				•	•			•	•	
Red-headed woodpecker		•		•	•	•	•	•	•		•	
Red-winged blackbird		•			•		•					•
Rose-breasted grosbeak	•	•	•		•		•	•	•	•	•	
Ruby-crowned kinglet						•	•	•		•	•	
Rufous-sided towhee		•		•	•		•					•
Scrub jay		•		•	•	•	•	•	•	•	•	
Song sparrow		•	•	•	•		•			•		•
Starling			•	•	•	•	•	•	•		•	
Summer tanager		•			•	•	•	•	•	•	•	
Tufted titmouse		•				•	•	•		•	•	
Varied thrush					•		•	•	•			•
White-breasted nuthatch	•	•		•	•	•	•	•		•	•	
White-crowned sparrow		•		•	•	•	•	•	•	•		•
White-throated sparrow		•	•	•	•	•	•	•				•
Yellow-bellied sapsucker		•				•	•	•	•	•	•	
Yellow-breasted chat							•	•	•		•	

*Mixed seed is defined here as being composed of 90% millet. Other ingredients—such as milo, wheat, cracked corn, and canary seed—compose the remaining 10%.

Squirrelproofing

Squirrels are delightful animals that can be just as enjoyable to watch as birds. Unfortunately, compared to birds, squirrels are voracious eaters and can empty a feeder in a short time. Because squirrels like most of the same foods as birds, they can become troublesome pests at bird feeders. However, they can be diverted by offering them their own feeder, and they can be kept from raiding bird feeders by using a variety of devices.

A squirrel feeding station placed at some distance from bird feeding stations will help keep squirrels from raiding the birds' food. Corn is an inexpensive squirrel food. Skewer an ear of dried corn on a nail driven up through the middle of a platform, or insert a screw eye into one end of a cob and hang the cob from a hook where squirrels can reach it. Many different squirrel feeders are available from the same dealers that sell bird feeders. Some of these feeders force the squirrels to perform amusing antics for their food.

Squirrels are agile and persistent acrobats. They can jump upward as much as 4 feet, and horizontally as much as 8 feet. They can balance on a wire and can climb anything that gives them the slightest grip. To protect a bird feeder mounted on a pole, place the pole at least 8 feet from anything the squirrel could use as a launching platform for a long leap to the feeder. Keep squirrels from climbing the pole by installing a metal or plastic barricade at least 4 feet above the ground. Make the barricade by wrapping sheet metal around the pole, in a cone shape, with the open end of the cone facing down. Or purchase a plastic or metal barricade made for this purpose.

Hanging feeders can be squirrelproofed with a commercially available plastic guard hung from the wire above the feeder. If your feeder is hung from a horizontal wire between two points, keep squirrels from walking on the wire by covering it with plastic tubing, such as PVC irrigation pipe, for several feet on each side of the feeder. The tubing will spin under the squirrel's feet, dumping the animal off the wire.

Many squirrelproof bird feeders are available. Most keep squirrels out, but some are unattractive and some restrict your view of the birds feeding. If you wish to place a feeder in a tree or another place that gives squirrels easy access, however, a squirrelproof feeder is the only way to keep squirrels from raiding the birds' food.

Recommended Storage Times for Bird Foods

	One Month	Two Months	Three Months	Six Months
Niger seed	•			
Cracked corn	•			
Sunflower meats	•			
Nutmeats		•		
Black oil sunflower seed			•	
Striped sunflower seed				•
Safflower seed				•
Millet, milo, or canary seed				•

products, how much to buy, and how to store them are important considerations.

Purchase birdseed from a reputable supplier. If you don't know of a source, check the ads in one of the magazines listed on page 92. There may be an outlet near you, or you can order through the mail.

Purchasing food in bulk is more economical than purchasing small amounts, but bulk purchasing requires ample storage space and involves the risk of damage from insects or dampness. Fortunately, many suppliers have sales at which you can purchase large amounts at a time and store it at the supplier's location; you take delivery of small portions, only as you need them. You save money and at the same time get fresh, safe food.

Inspect newly purchased seed for insect damage. Tiny round holes in hulls are signs that the grain weevil is present and that some of the larvae have already hatched. The larvae of this pest eat the kernel and leave only the empty hull. Another insect, the grain moth, leaves webby strands at points where the bag holding the seeds is sewn together. If you find signs of either of these pests, return the seed and ask for a fresh supply.

Store seed in a trash can with a tight lid, in a cool, dry spot. Because grain moths could hatch and escape the seed bin, avoid storing seed near other foods. A garage or unheated porch makes an appropriate storage site.

Seeds and grains will last much longer in cool temperatures than warm temperatures and under dry conditions than damp conditions. Regardless of the conditions where you live, do not store food for longer than six months. If food becomes moldy or shows signs of serious insect damage, throw it out. Clean and disinfect the seed container before using it to store a fresh supply of seed.

Once the food has been placed in a feeder, it is subject to even greater hazards, particularly if birds do not eat it quickly. Food that is in open trays or on the ground is the most subject to spoilage and contamination from droppings. To avoid health problems, offer small amounts at a time and clean these areas frequently. Trays are easier to clean than the open ground.

Tubular feeders that hang from a branch or some other support offer the best protection from moisture and contamination. Hanging feeders with adjustable overhead domes also

Weevil damage to sunflower seed.

Grain moth larva and webbing in a bag of sunflower seed.

provide good protection from the elements and are reasonably squirrelproof.

Wooden hopper feeders, either hanging or on posts or platforms, are reasonably safe if all the food sifts out as birds eat their way through the supply. But if some of the food is left behind inside the hopper, it will decay and lead to a possible health hazard. All feeders, regardless of the make, should be easy to clean.

The bird foods that you need to be most careful with are niger seed, cracked corn, sunflower meats (and all "no-waste" mixes), black oil sunflower seed, and nutmeats. These seeds and nutmeats lack a tight outer covering, a fact that makes them susceptible to insect damage and spoilage.

Niger seed spoils quickly when exposed to moisture. Even the condensation inside a tube-type feeder will cause spoilage. If birds are no longer coming to feeders holding niger seed, the seed may have gone bad. Empty the feeder, clean it, and offer a fresh supply.

Problems of spoilage at the feeder or on the ground are all but eliminated if birds eat the food quickly. By keeping limited amounts of bird food on hand and by offering only limited amounts at a time, you can overcome spoilage and contamination problems.

KEEPING THE PEACE

For many who are feeding birds for the first time, it comes as a surprise to discover that playing host to birds calls for mediation skills. You may have to keep the peace among birds as well as negotiate with neighbors.

Bird Arbitration

Many birds, including some favorites, take more than their share. Squirrels and chipmunks will do the same if you let them. It is necessary to discourage some visitors and encourage those you prefer by selecting and offering food carefully. Preventing a few unpopular species from interfering with your feeding program can be difficult and take patience. Be willing to experiment; vary the foods, feeders, and feeder placement until you achieve the desired balance. The chart beginning on page 75 lists over 70 species of birds that most people like and ways to attract them.

Relationships with Neighbors

Bird-feeding activities might cause problems with human neighbors, who complain about the birds that flock to the area or the debris from bird feeders. There is really not much you can do about people who simply do not like birds. But if the birds are making a nuisance of themselves by spattering cars and laundry with their droppings, it is advisable to take steps. The best solution is to plant a fast-growing

Top: Some birders enjoy blue jays and their aggressive ways; others dislike them. To control disruption by blue jays, fill a feeder with their favorite foods and place it at a distance from other bird feeders. Bottom: Offering food from a second-story apartment can create a problem. Birds are messy eaters and the area below the feeder may become covered with litter. Hulled sunflower seeds or "no-mess" mixes help solve this problem.

evergreen hedge between yourself and the complaining neighbor. A high latticework fence will also help. Birds use the most open approaches to fly into and leave an area. Tall barriers will help keep them out of the neighbor's yard. A barrier will also stop debris from feeders from reaching points beyond your home ground.

Those who live in high-rises and feed birds at windowsills or on balconies have an obligation to minimize the debris that falls to lower levels. Do this by offering only seeds that have had their hulls removed. For a little extra cost, buy sunflower meats or no-waste mixtures. Sweep up droppings and debris daily.

WINDOW STRIKES

Discovering a dead or injured bird that has collided with a window is distressing. Window strikes can happen whether or not you are feeding birds. They may see the reflection of a tree or shrub in a window and fly toward it, mistaking it for a place to land. Windows that reveal windows on the other side of a house are particularly dangerous. To birds, these look like passageways through which they can fly. Mortality at such windows can be especially heavy. Windows are as damaging to fit birds as unfit ones.

If you find a bird that is only stunned, place it in a paper bag, twist the top, and give it time to recover. When you hear it moving, take it to a door or window and release it.

The list that follows presents a few ways to prevent window strikes.

•Place feeders in or very close to windows or 25 feet or more away from windows. Birds that feed at windows become aware that the glass is a barrier. Also, if they take off close to a window when startled, they can't gain enough momentum to harm themselves.

•Silhouettes of hawks or owls placed on the glass are commonly used to warn birds away from windows. This method gives mixed results.

•Anything that makes the window look less like a passageway will reduce the incidence of window strikes. This can include placing ribbons, tinsel, or bells outside the window or placing strips of tape on the window.

•The most effective method is to screen the window with netting. Hang bird netting (the kind used to protect fruit trees from birds) from the eaves or just outside the window. If the bottom is weighted or attached to something to keep the netting taut, it is almost invisible.

Protecting Your Guests

A birdwatcher occasionally sees a sick bird at the feeder. The bird moves slowly and stays behind when other birds fly away. The appearance of such a bird serves as a warning: Ask yourself if conditions at the feeder could be the cause of the illness. Where birds congregate and bird droppings accumulate, unsanitary conditions can foster the spread of disease. By taking precautions to eliminate unsanitary conditions or moldy food, you can prevent the outbreak of several bird diseases.

Unsafe Foods

Messy foods, such as kitchen leftovers or overripe fruit, can lead to unsanitary conditions and can attract pests of various kinds. Limit the use of these foods, or present them carefully in a feeder protected from pests. Leave them out for only a short time, and clean the feeder frequently.

Suet can be a hazardous food in summer. If the suet becomes soft and begins to liquify in hot weather, it can mat the breast and chin feathers of some birds, such as woodpeckers. This problem can be avoided by using the appropriate suet mixture for summer and presenting it properly.

Birds need fewer carbohydrates in summer but still need as much protein and as many vitamins and minerals as ever. Research in regard to the seasonal needs of birds has yielded some interesting specifics. British researchers have found that nestling titmice are unable to digest fat (particularly mutton fat) and that oil-rich peanuts and coconuts were also harmful to young in their early stages of development. In light of this research, do not offer peanuts or coconut in summer. Furthermore, peanuts soon become rancid in hot, wet weather.

The seeds of sunflower, safflower, and niger, and mixed birdseeds that do not contain peanuts, are appropriate summertime offerings. But, as is true the year round, these foods must be fresh and free from mold. Use corn in its various forms sparingly in summer. It is a food that elevates body temperature. In addition, it spoils easily.

For the most part, birds instinctively know what is good for them and avoid foods that are harmful. Whatever they receive at our feeders is balanced by foods they obtain in the wild. When birds find an unfamiliar food at a feeder, they wait a long time before sampling it. They may not be so astute, however, in detecting rot or mold in a familiar food. Humans must take the responsibility for ensuring that food offered in feeders is safe and appropriate.

Sometimes you must look beyond the feeder to ensure a safe food supply. The bright red or orange berries of firethorn or pyracantha that stay on the bush all winter have a way of fermenting. The birds that eat them can become intoxicated. This most frequently happens in January or February when a warm spell is followed by cold weather. American robins and cedar waxwings, are the most often affected. They become woozy, often flying into houses or into oncoming traffic. Residents of California have come to expect these binges at about the same time every winter; the same sights are seen wherever pyracantha is commonly grown.

Other fruits that ferment and cause similar problems are those of the apple tree, wild black cherry, Brazilian pepper (*Schinus terebinthifolius*), Chinaberry (*Melia azedarach*), and mountain ash (*Sorbus* species). One way to reduce consumption of fermented fruit is to drape bushes with bird netting as soon as intoxication is noted. Netting is available at most garden centers. But this helps to only a limited degree. Simply wait a while and the problem will disappear.

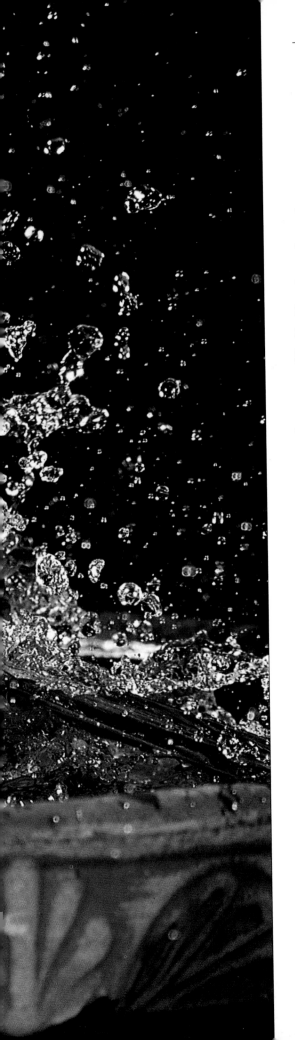

Providing Water

Water—in a fountain, pool, or birdbath—is as irresistible to birds as it is to people. Here are easy ways to provide fresh water in your garden the year around.

A reliable source of fresh water is an essential ingredient in any bird-attracting program. Many species of birds that don't eat the specialized foods provided in a feeder may be drawn to the yard or garden by water. In the arid parts of the West, water is a scarce resource for birds; it is the most important thing you can offer to attract them. Even in the moist Northeast and Northwest, water in the form birds prefer can be hard to find. Especially during long dry spells and in winter when water is frozen, birds may have a long search for a chance to drink and bathe.

There are many ways to provide water for birds while enhancing the beauty of the home landscape. Artificial "rain puddles," or birdbaths, are available in a huge variety of sizes, forms, and materials. If you have a garden pool, it can be adapted to the special needs of birds. If you're starting from scratch, a simple pool is easily constructed. A plastic tub, an old wine barrel or bathtub, a scooped-out log, a simple hole in the ground lined with plastic, or a garden hose with a mist sprayer can entice birds to use the water you provide.

A source of water can be the setting for birds' most active displays. This immature cardinal discovers the delights of ostentatious bathing.

FRESH WATER THE YEAR AROUND

However you present it, water should be fresh, clean, and abundant. Hose off and refill birdbaths often. In hot weather, check them daily to make sure they are full. Periodically clean and refill garden pools. A circulating pump and the cooperation of fish and plants will help keep the water fresh and clear. Water intended for birds is no place for chemicals of any kind. Never add chemicals to it to control algae or insects or to prevent freezing.

Water should be available and accessible in all seasons. One of the prime attractions of water you provide is its reliability; natural sources tend to shift, dry up, or freeze with changing weather. The birdbath is popular even in the coldest days of winter, and it's important to keep it unfrozen. Birdbaths and very small pools can be thawed by pouring a kettle of boiling water in them, but this is tedious to do on a regular basis.

The most convenient way to keep birdbath water from freezing is to use an immersion water heater designed specifically for outdoor use. Several varieties are available in garden-supply stores and hardware centers. Some are designed for water deeper than that usually found in birdbaths and are more appropriate for pools and tubs. For the shallow water of a birdbath or small garden pool, purchase a version to operate at a depth of 1½ to 3 inches. It should have an automatic thermostat that shuts off the heating element when the water reaches 40° F. If an extension cord is needed, be sure to use the heavy-duty exterior kind with a triple-pronged, grounded plug. Heating tapes are also available for use in birdbaths, but they are appropriate only in mild climates with occasional freezes.

An alternative to placing a water heater in the birdbath is to buy a bath with a heating unit already installed and completely hidden. You can plug the bath into an electrical outlet whenever temperatures drop below freezing. Both pedestal and dish baths having this feature are available at wild-bird centers and garden stores.

An immersion heater keeps water just warm enough to prevent freezing.

Birds prefer water only a couple of inches deep. Most, like this chickadee, can't swim and need to stand on the bottom to bathe.

Accessibility

The surface of the container, where birds enter the water, should be rough to provide sure footing. Textured materials appropriate for birdbaths, pools, and streams include sand, stone, pebbles, and concrete. You can make smooth, slippery surfaces such as plastic or metal more attractive to birds by using coarse sandpaper to roughen them or attaching the kind of textured footing used in bathtubs.

The water container should have a gradual, shallow slope. Almost all garden birds are fearful of water deeper than 2 to 3 inches, and some like it even shallower than that. Don't buy a birdbath any deeper than 3 inches, and select one that approaches this depth very gradually. The depth should increase only 1 inch in 8 inches. A lip or other perch where birds can alight before entering the water is an advantage, as is a dry flat space on which they can hop to the edge of the water.

Safety and Visibility

Safety is a prime consideration in placing a water source. A wet bird, preoccupied with bathing and slowed by wet feathers, is a vulnerable target for cats. The water source should be out in the open, with no close shrubs behind which a predatory cat can lurk or overhanging limbs it can pounce from. Most birds prefer a high perch and dense cover about 15 feet away from the water so that they can examine the area for possible danger and return to a refuge for preening. A few birds, however (especially birds of the forest floor, such as thrushes), prefer secret forest pools and quiet streams that are close to cover. These shy birds are more likely to visit a birdbath or garden pool hidden in dense shrubbery.

Height gives added protection to birds. If your birdbath is near dense vegetation, raise it off the ground about 3 feet. Out in the open, ground-level birdbaths and pools are acceptable. A cat that is exposed rarely gets close enough to be a threat to birds.

Be sure to place the birds' water source in a spot that is visible and convenient for you. Establish it near a place you use a lot, such as the house, patio, or quiet sitting area. Don't mask your line of sight with dense vegetation. Water for the birds should be as close to a faucet as possible, so you don't have to lug heavy coils of hose for cleaning and refilling.

Top: An elevated birdbath near shrubs or trees provides safety from lurking predators and offers nearby perches on which to dry off.
Bottom: A robin enjoys a dip in a backyard pool lined with flagstone.

WAYS TO SUPPLY WATER

How you decide to provide water for birds will depend on the time and expense you wish to spend rigging the water supply, the time you are willing to devote to maintenance, and what you find appropriate and beautiful for your yard or garden.

Birdbaths

A birdbath is the easiest way to set up a water source for birds. Birdbaths are available in a variety of ornamental styles that range from simple, naturalistic containers of stone or wood, to colorful, elaborate sculptures. Don't buy a birdbath with moving, shiny parts that might frighten birds. Otherwise, give your aesthetic sense free rein.

One aspect of birdbath design is the type of support the container receives. Some birdbaths are simple dishes to set on the ground or on a windowsill or deck. Some hang by chains from a balcony, eave, or wall bracket. Others attach to a window with suction cups. The most common type is set on a pedestal, which raises it about 3 feet off the ground. Heavy stone, ceramic, or concrete dishes should have a broad, sturdy support. Metal, plastic, or wooden birdbaths should be firmly anchored to the pedestal or be of single-piece construction.

As long as its edge slopes gradually, the size of the basin is not crucial. However, anything less than 12 inches across is generally too small, and baths or pools less than 18 inches in diameter will usually be used by only one bird at a time. Most birdbaths are 24 to 36 inches in diameter. This seems to be a good size for community bathing.

Birdbaths are available in a wide variety of materials. Terra-cotta and glazed ceramic birdbaths are attractive, but crack easily when water freezes in winter. Concrete and cement birdbaths are the most common available, and their rough texture is a decided advantage. The solid, heavy construction of concrete

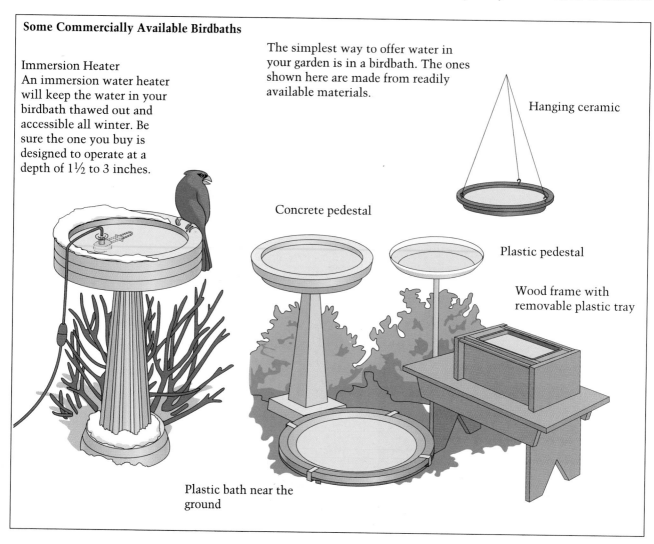

Some Commercially Available Birdbaths

Immersion Heater
An immersion water heater will keep the water in your birdbath thawed out and accessible all winter. Be sure the one you buy is designed to operate at a depth of 1½ to 3 inches.

The simplest way to offer water in your garden is in a birdbath. The ones shown here are made from readily available materials.

Hanging ceramic

Concrete pedestal

Plastic pedestal

Wood frame with removable plastic tray

Plastic bath near the ground

withstands freezing better than terra-cotta, glazed ceramic, or cement. (Cement is concrete without reinforcing gravel.)

Plastic and metal birdbaths withstand all kinds of weather, but their surfaces are too slippery unless the surface is textured. Their light weight makes them easy to handle but requires a firm, solid support to keep them from tipping. Metal birdbaths should be made of stainless steel or coated with rust-resistant paint. Painted metal birdbaths will eventually chip and flake, and will need occasional repainting.

A few birdbaths sold commercially are made entirely of wood. They are difficult to keep clean, and even those made from long-lasting wood, such as redwood or cedar, won't last as long as other kinds of birdbaths. They are generally well liked by birds, however, and can be very attractive.

With a little imagination you can easily make your own birdbath. Any kind of dish with a gradual slope, a lip for perching, and the appropriate depth and dimensions can be used. The kind of saucer usually placed under large potted plants can make an excellent tiny birdbath. A 3-foot log, cut square on both ends, makes a good pedestal. A close-grained log,

Top: A birdbath can be as simple as a rock with a depression for holding water. Some natural material, such as this volcanic stone, is soft enough to work easily with hand tools; if you can't find a stone with a suitable depression, you can make one.
Bottom: Hanging birdbaths are attractive and popular. Birds seem to prefer those that hang near the ground.

Easy Garden Pools

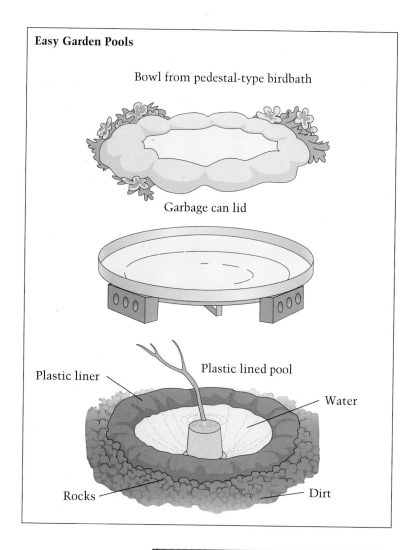

Bowl from pedestal-type birdbath

Garbage can lid

Plastic liner

Plastic lined pool

Water

Rocks

Dirt

such as one of oak or hickory, can be hollowed out with a chisel to contain water. A large stone that has a natural depression to hold water can be an attractive addition to your garden.

When birds bathe, particularly in large numbers at a time, they can get quite excited and energetic, splashing water all about. Unless you want a soggy, muddy area around the bath, set it on a pad that will quickly absorb or drain off water. Gravel or sand drains well. For a 30-inch birdbath, remove about 4 inches of soil from an area about 4 feet square. Refill the depression with gravel or sand. Set the birdbath in place so that it is level. Dark-colored river gravel, pea gravel, or sand is attractive.

Small Pools

A small pool useful to birds can be nothing more than a birdbath set into the ground. Some simple pools can even be large enough for a few fish and water plants.

The easiest kind of small pool to provide is the basin of a birdbath; heavy concrete ones work best. Dig a depression deep enough so that the lip of the basin extends about 2 inches from ground level. The lip will prevent soil from washing in. Set the basin in place, backfill around the edges, and you have a small garden pool in a matter of minutes.

This garden pool is lined with flexible PVC fabric sold for the purpose. Small stones line the edges and bottom of the pool. An inexpensive pump in the bottom circulates water through a tube and out the bamboo pipe.

To build a small garden pool whose basin is the earth itself, begin by digging out the soil to any depth and shape you wish. Use some of the earth you dig up to build a small mound about 6 inches higher than ground level and about 12 inches wide all the way around the edge. Tamp the soil in the depression and compress the mounded edge. While you are tamping, create a small trench in the mound around the hole. The trench should be about 4 inches deep and 6 inches back from the mound. Then line the hole with a heavy sheet of polyethylene, plastic, or rubber, allowing its edges to extend outside the perimeter by about a foot. Fold the excess down into the trench, and cover it with gravel. You are ready to fill your pool with water. Black or dark brown plastic is more attractive and less noticeable than a light color. You can hide the plastic by scattering gravel on the bottom of the pool and lining the sides and top of the edges with small flat rocks set carefully in place so they don't tear the plastic. This also helps to hold the lining in place.

A bit more expensive, but also more permanent, is a ready-made pool of fiberglass or plastic. Such pools are available at garden centers and hardware stores. Simply dig out soil to accommodate the shape of the pool, set the pool in place, and fill it with water.

Top: This elaborate pool is made the same way as the pool on the facing page. The shallow water and stones near the edge provide easy access for birds.
Bottom: Put birdbaths where you can watch the spectacular splashing of feathered bathers.

Moving Water in the Garden

Dripping hose

Bucket with hole

Birdbath fountain

Musical, Moving Water

The sound of gently moving water is extremely appealing to birds. In fact, bird-banders often lure them with dripping water. Audible water in the garden can be provided by a simple dripping hose or by a sophisticated waterfall that requires complex plumbing. However you supply it, remember that a little water music goes a long way. A thunderous waterfall or a huge erupting fountain will frighten more birds than it attracts. Small drips, tinkles, and bubbles are what birds like.

A simple dripper can be made with a small-diameter clear plastic tube that runs up the trunk of a tree and out a low-hanging branch over the birdbath. An adapter will enable you to connect the tubing to the garden hose and disconnect it easily when you need the hose for other purposes. A shutoff clamp with an adjustable screw attached to the outflow end of the tube will allow precise regulation of the water flow.

Many birds love to fly through mist and fine sprays. Hang a hose with the nozzle set on mist spray over a tree branch or some other raised support. Or use a soaker hose that emits mist or fine streams of water. Turn the water on regularly at a set time of day, and birds will quickly

Many birds enjoy a sprinkler. This scrub jay seizes the opportunity for a quick bath.

learn when to expect this treat. Hummingbirds are very fond of bathing this way.

Fountains and waterfalls in the home landscape are as pleasing to people as they are to birds. Some birdbaths are equipped with fountains and jet sprays that bubble or spray up from the center of the pool. A simple waterfall can be constructed as a series of basins, with water falling from one to another. Whether you buy a kit or purchase the necessary hardware separately, make sure that the basin is deep enough to keep the pump out of sight and covered with water.

Natural-looking waterfalls and streams require some artistry and technical expertise to build. They can add an exciting dimension to your yard or garden, however, and many people consider hiring a professional landscape architect for this job. Remember, though, that shallow areas and a gentle flow of water are the keys to attracting birds.

If you want to build a waterfall yourself, keep it small and simple. An easy one is based on the same principle as the birdbath basin dug into the ground. On a sloping hillside, dig in a series of basins so that they overlap, one above the other, in stairstep fashion. Pay special attention to the angle and sharpness of each lip over which the water will flow. The idea is to prevent water from flowing or dripping back up under the basin, loosening soil and washing it into the system. The lip should be sharp and at a slight downward tilt so that water falls cleanly over the edge.

The bottom pool, or a hidden chamber adjacent to it, should be deep enough to hold a pump. Clear flexible plastic tubing will return the water from the bottom basin back to the top. Hide the tubing by burying it in the ground or growing plants over it. The size of the pump you need will be determined by the intended rate of flow (which should be slow, for the birds' sake) and by how much higher the top basin is than the lowest one.

Consider carefully the placement of any birdbath, fountain, pool, or waterfall that requires electricity. Using extension cords as permanent outdoor garden fixtures is unwise. In many areas local law prohibits such use. Since your fountain, birdbath, or pool is a permanent outdoor fixture, consider hiring an electrician who will run a line out to it and install a switch inside the house. The safety and convenience of such a setup are well worth the expense. Such a line can also power attractive lighting or the water heater you might use in winter to keep the water flowing and the birds splashing.

A Simple Waterfall

A series of basins dug into a sloping hillside, with a pump to recirculate the water, makes a simple attractive waterfall

A leaking hose provides drinking water for this female cardinal.

Providing Housing

Birdhouses of specific shapes and dimensions attract specific birds. In this chapter you'll find a plan for a basic birdhouse to build, with variations for different birds.

What a quiet, sad season spring would be without the music of birds. Proclaiming their territory and courting their mates, many of our favorite birds announce the start of their busiest season. Their elaborate territorial stakeouts and courtship rituals are only the beginning. Selecting a nesting site; collecting nesting materials and building a nest (which can take thousands of trips over a week or more); laying eggs and patiently incubating them; nurturing, feeding, warming, and protecting the helpless nestlings that emerge; and leading the infants to maturity—all these are jobs that will completely occupy the busy parents for the summer months.

Many factors affect a bird's choice of a nesting site, and most of them are beyond human control. You can do much, however, to encourage birds to nest in your yard or garden. The most important thing to remember: Be patient. Birds may take a while—several seasons, even—to discover your efforts.

Some birds are especially territorial during the breeding season. The size of a breeding territory varies with the species, from many square miles for some birds of prey to less than an acre for the American robin and red-winged blackbird. For some birds that nest in communities, such as purple martins, the "territory," if it can be called that, may be only a few inches. The size of a territory can fluctuate from individual to individual within a species, depending on competition, population level, and available food and nesting sites. Some birds, such as mockingbirds, defend their territories with extraordinary zeal, attacking intruding birds and other creatures (including cats and humans) much larger than themselves.

Unless you live on property of estate dimensions, you will probably not attract more than one pair of a territorial species; each pair will drive away all competing individuals of its kind. Of course, your land may straddle a territorial boundary, and birdfeeders may attract several

On the way to her nest, a Carolina wren pauses with a beakful of dry grass.

pairs from adjacent territories. However, because they prefer different feeding and nesting sites, different species can and often do nest in surprising proximity, and it is quite possible to have a number of nesting pairs of different kinds of birds raising their young in the same small yard.

To increase the number of breeding pairs in your yard or garden, provide what this book has recommended throughout: diversity. The greater the number of types of plants, birdhouses, and nesting materials you provide, the greater the variety of nesting birds that will be drawn to your outdoor space. Ten birdhouses of the same style and dimensions in one garden may draw only a single pair of birds while the other nine birdhouses remain empty.

This chapter will describe the kinds of birdhouses and other shelters you can provide for birds in your home landscape. For specific information on dimensions of birdhouses, including the diameters of entrances, see the chart on page 72.

NESTING MATERIALS

By providing suitable nesting materials you can offer a powerful inducement for birds to nest in your yard or garden. A single nest often consists of a thousand or even several thousand

Nesting Materials

Empty suet feeder

Suspended wire basket

Bicycle basket

pieces, each requiring an individual search-and-carry mission. Particularly in super-tidy areas—where every dead twig is pruned off and thrown away, where every mown blade or loose leaf is swept up into a plastic bag—the lack of nesting materials can remove your outdoor area from consideration as a nest site.

Offer nesting materials in concentrated, readily observable piles and stashes. By concentrating the offerings, you reduce the time it takes a bird to find things and build a nest. Even if all you offer is a bundle of dead twigs, putting them in one spot can be of significant value to birds. Empty suet feeders and wire baskets hung from a branch or nailed to a tree are excellent means for offering nesting materials; these containers are convenient for the birds, and the wind can't scatter the materials. If you offer loose nesting materials, place them in a conspicuous spot out in the open, such as on the lawn or draped over a clothesline.

Cut stringy materials into lengths no longer than 8 inches. When looped and woven into a nest, longer pieces of string, yarn, and such have caused entanglement and even strangulation. Don't place materials directly in a birdhouse, which will make it look as though it is already occupied. Remember that any of these items that aren't used by birds become litter if not kept in a restricted area.

Several birds—including American robins, wood thrushes, eastern phoebes, and barn and cliff swallows—require mud to construct their nests. You can assist and encourage them to nest nearby if you keep a supply of mud handy during the nest-building season. Not too much is necessary—a garbage can lid sunk into an out-of-the-way corner, kept full of wet, sticky clay soil, is plenty.

BIRDHOUSES

About fifty species of North American birds are known to use birdhouses for nesting. The ones most likely to nest in the home landscape are listed in the chart on page 72. Except for house finches, most of these birds naturally nest in cavities or crevices, rather than constructing nests on tree limbs, in shrubs, or on the ground. In many areas, the practice of "clean" forestry, agriculture, and gardening has severely reduced the availability of old, decaying trees that can be used as nesting sites. You can assist by supplying "cavities" in the form of birdhouses. A wide variety of commercially made birdhouses is available for purchase from hardware stores, garden centers, and mail-order firms advertised in such magazines as *Audubon.* Some birdhouses are ready-made, others come in easy-to-assemble kits. Or you can make your own—an easy, inexpensive, and interesting project.

The Basic Birdhouse

The illustration accompanying this section presents a design for a birdhouse you can build yourself. This design is adaptable to accommodate nearly all cavity-nesting birds; consult the chart on page 72 for the dimensions appropriate to the species of bird you wish to attract. In building or buying a birdhouse, keep the following points in mind.

•A birdhouse should be designed and built for a particular species. A house said to appeal to a wide variety may appeal to none—or to the wrong ones. When purchasing a birdhouse, always ask for one that will suit a specific bird; ask for a house wren box or a northern flicker house, for example. The style and construction of birdhouses for different species can be very similar; the important difference is in the dimensions. The diameter and placement of the entrance hole, and the depth, width, and height of the interior (including available floor space) are the important dimensions to know. Nevertheless, many species are close enough in their favored dimensions that the bird you get may not be the one you expected.

•Except for purple martin houses, a birdhouse should be designed for a single nest. "Duplexes" and "triplexes" are a waste of effort and materials,because a bird's territorial tendencies will prevent occupancy of more than one cavity.

•In general the simplest, plainest design, painted or stained a subdued color, will be the most attractive to birds. Many commercially built birdhouses, and designs for building your own, are loaded with useless doodads and frills. These cute birdhouses are designed more for garden decoration than for bird attraction. Especially avoid birdhouses with parts that move in the wind and houses made of highly reflective materials.

•Material for birdhouse construction should be weather-resistant, durable, and "breathe" well. Such material will allow the house to last

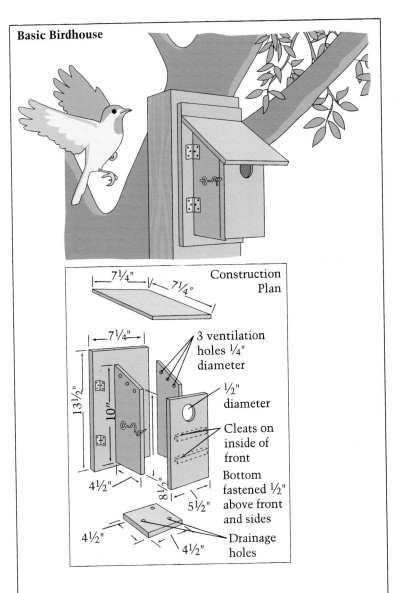

Basic Birdhouse

Construction Plan

3 ventilation holes 1/4" diameter

1/2" diameter

Cleats on inside of front

Bottom fastened 1/2" above front and sides

Drainage holes

7 1/4" · 7 1/4"

7 1/4"

13 1/2" 10"

4 1/2"

8 1/2"

5 1/2"

4 1/2"   4 1/2"

The roof of the birdhouse should carry away water. It needs to be sloping, and should overlap the front and sides by at least 1½". It is best not to hinge the roof for opening and cleaning, as the hinge is difficult to seal against the rain. Hinge one of the sides instead. One inch back from the front edge of the roof, score a drip line 1/8" deep on the underside, to keep water from running into the seams and entrance. Do not attach a perch on the outside of the entrance. Birds don't need it, and it will only help squirrels and cats to raid the nest. However, on the inside, just below the entrance hole, attach one or two small, horizontal cleats to assist the parents and the young in their exit. A series of horizontal cuts 1/8" deep will serve the same purpose. Good ventilation is essential to prevent heat buildup. At the top of each side, drill three 1/4" holes for ventilation. The ventilation holes should always be drilled above the level of the entrance hole to avoid drafts. One side of the birdhouse should be removable or hinged to permit removal of old nests and cleaning after the nestlings have left. However, the opening side must be able to be locked firmly in place while the box is in use. The bottom should have good drainage in case water gets into the box during a storm. Unless drainage is otherwise provided for, drill three 1/4" holes into the bottom of the box.

Some Commercially Available Birdhouses

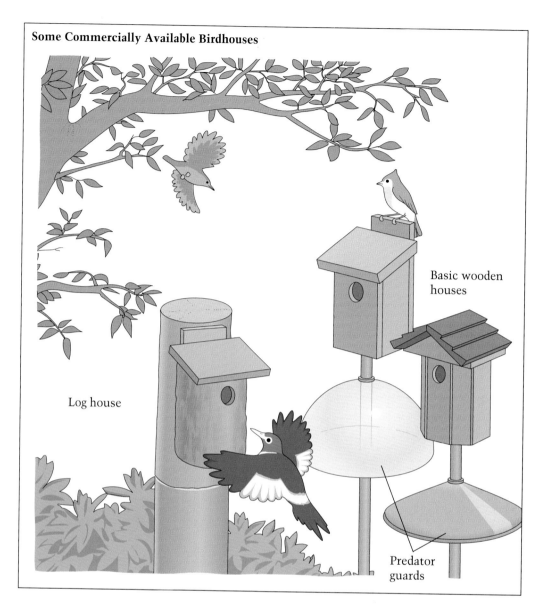

Basic wooden houses

Log house

Predator guards

several years and stay dry inside, with no moisture buildup. Birdhouses should be well insulated so they remain warm on cool days and cool on hot days. The latter is especially important, because many birds prefer that their houses be placed in open, sunny spots. About the only construction material that meets these standards is wood ¾ inch to 1 inch thick. Birdhouse fasteners should be galvanized steel or brass hardware (nails, screws, hinges, and clasps). Among the woods that are the most durable and easiest to work with are redwood, white cedar, and cypress. Lumber should be well seasoned, since green or wet wood will warp and split. Avoid plastic houses, because moisture will build up inside. Avoid houses made of metal or ceramic materials, which may bake the baby birds. Exceptions are commercial aluminum houses made especially for

purple martins, which are designed to provide adequate circulation.

•If you wish to paint the birdhouse, use latex paint. Natural, dull colors—especially browns, grays, and greens—are best for attracting birds. White can be useful in keeping temperatures down in the hot sun, however, and many species of birds don't seem to mind it.

•The birdhouse mounting should be strong, secure, and stable. Loosely mounted boxes that can jiggle or sway in the wind or when a parent alights are not attractive to birds (except for wrens, which accept hanging houses) and court possible disaster. If a birdhouse presents even the slightest chance of coming loose and falling to the ground, it is a potential deathtrap. The two most common ways of mounting a birdhouse are on top of a post or sturdy pole, or nailed (or, preferably, screwed) to a vertical

A Special House for Purple Martins

Along with their melodius calls, graceful flight, and diet of tens of thousands of flying insects, the interesting social behavior of purple martins makes attracting these birds well worth the effort.

Formerly, the only way you could have a purple martin house was to build one yourself—a complicated project that frequently resulted in heavy structures that were difficult to raise or lower and inconvenient to take apart and maintain. If you are a confirmed do-it-yourselfer and have the experience and equipment to do the job, you may enjoy building one yourself. The best plan for a martin house is available from the Superintendent of Documents, U.S. Government Printing Office, Washington, DC 20402. Send $2.50 and ask for "Homes for Birds," Conservation Bulletin #14, Stock #024-010-00524-4.

In most cases metal nesting boxes are not recommended for birds. The only exception is for purple martins. Extensive testing has resulted in houses designed to provide air circulation and exceptional heat-reflecting capacity. When you evaluate designs for a purple martin house, make sure the one you choose has those characteristics. Commercially made aluminum martin houses have several advantages over homemade wooden ones. They are light, easy to put up and take down, and weather-resistant. Compared to wooden houses, they require less refinishing and maintenance. Whether you buy or build your own, your martin house should meet the requirements cited in the following list.

• Each nesting compartment of the martin house should be built to the correct dimensions (see the chart on page 72).

• The best martin houses are expandable so that you can add new floors and compartments as the colony grows from year to year. Houses have been built with over a hundred compartments, but it is best to start small, with 8 to 12.

• Place the house correctly. If you don't have a suitable location for a martin house, there is little chance it will be used. A martin house should be mounted on a pole 12 to 20 feet high, in an open lawn or meadow at least 40 feet from any tree, structure, or other flight obstruction. Even shrubs or small trees over 5 feet tall are a hindrance to these birds; they like to approach the nest in long gliding swoops. Nearby bodies of water and large, open lawns and meadows are a distinct plus because martins hunt insects on the wing and need large areas without flight obstructions to do so. Telephone or utility wires about 30 yards from the martin house are another advantage—the birds use them as perches.

Try to position the house within 100 feet of a human dwelling. Purple martins have learned to associate us with protection from enemies and therefore seem to prefer nesting close to our homes.

• The martin house should provide ventilation from holes cut into each compartment, above the entrance; a central air shaft that allows rising heat to escape through attic vents; or both.

• Because a martin house should be cleaned yearly, before the birds return in spring, you should be able to raise and lower it easily. Many aluminum houses feature a convenient pulley-and-winch apparatus that telescopes the pole and enables cleaning. Wooden houses should be stored under cover in winter.

• In offering housing for the first time to purple martins, it is important that the martins be the first birds to stake a claim. If other hole-nesting birds are already at hand, the martins will go elsewhere. A good way to exclude early comers is to use cups to block entrance holes. As soon as the martins arrive, remove the cups.

• White is the best color to use on a purple martin house. White reflects the heat of the sun and provides a sharp contrast with the dark entrance opening, thereby making the opening more visible to possible occupants.

support like a wall or post. Having the back piece extend at least 2 inches on the sides or top provides a convenient surface through which to nail up the house. It is important to know where and how you plan on securing the birdhouse before buying or building it.

• Weather protection is also important in mounting the birdhouse. The entrance hole should be directed away from the path of prevailing winds; in most places, this means facing south or southeast. Do not mount a birdhouse so that the entrance side faces up even slightly. If it is tilted up, it will collect rain. A slight downward tilt is best. When nailing or screwing a birdhouse to a wall or post, insert a small strip of wood on either side of the back, so that there is a space between the back and what it is mounted against. This will prevent water from collecting and soaking through the back piece.

Houses that Discourage Starlings and House Sparrows

Entrance holes 1½ inches or less in diameter will exclude starlings, but they need to be 1⅛ inches or less to exclude house sparrows. Unfortunately, this size also excludes many desirable birds. Another approach is to mount birdhouses just as the desired species is returning in the spring. This is effective only with birds like purple martins, which are faithful to

A bluebird house on a fence post. Some bird lovers provide and maintain many such houses.

the same nesting spot year after year. In addition, the approach requires close observation and readiness on your part.

Housing for Bluebirds

Bluebirds are among the most sought-after birdhouse tenants. Mountain and western bluebirds are found in the West; eastern bluebirds are found in the East. Not only are these colorful birds cheerful guests, but they are in need of "artificial" nesting sites. Since around 1900 the number of bluebirds has dropped sharply because of competition from European starlings and house sparrows, species that choose nesting sites similar to the bluebird's. At the same time, clean farming has deprived all birds of the dead trees and rotting fenceposts where they used to find cavities for nesting.

With more people building bluebird houses in recent years, bluebirds are making a remarkable comeback. Throughout much of North America, thousands of bluebird houses have been placed in yards, parks, and along roads and highways.

Some bluebird landlords supervise hundreds of boxes, which they have placed at intervals near highways and back roads. The houses are usually attached to fenceposts and spaced about 200 feet apart. The habitat can be a pasture, cultivated field, or sparsely wooded area. (Always obtain the permission of the landowner before placing a birdhouse on his or her land.)

Although bluebirds are no longer found in heavily built-up districts, they still inhabit residential areas close to parks, golf courses, and open fields. Anyone living in such neighborhoods has a good chance of attracting bluebirds. Once bluebirds accept a house, they are likely to come back year after year. Houses that were used for nesting in summer are often used at night for roosting.

For the proper dimensions of a bluebird house, see the chart on page 72. White, gray, brown, or green are suitable colors for such a house. To facilitate inspection, the house should be easy to open. Birds are less disturbed if the house is opened at the top. The recommended 1½-inch diameter entrance hole will keep out starlings but not house sparrows. If house sparrows enter a house with bluebird eggs or young, they will promptly destroy whatever they find (even, occasionally, an adult).

Remove a house sparrow nest. Indeed, it is best not to place bluebird houses in areas where house sparrows are abundant. Otherwise, you will have a constant and, often, a losing battle to keep the sparrows under control. As for other tenants—such as wrens, swallows, chickadees, titmice, and nuthatches—treasure them as much as bluebirds. Like bluebirds, they consume harmful insects and are in need of extra housing.

Whether your bluebird house is in a residential area or farming country, inspect it weekly during the time that bluebirds are looking for nesting sites. In addition to ejecting house sparrows, check for vandalism (not uncommon in some areas) and such unwelcome guests as ants and wasps. Bluebirds won't nest in a house that has a wasp nest attached to the ceiling or sides. A coating of grease on the ceiling will help prevent wasps from building. A dusting of rotenone or sulfur when the house is unoccupied will discourage lice and other insect pests. As soon as the young have left, remove the old nest and any infertile eggs. This will clear the way for subsequent broods. Bluebirds sometimes nest two or three times in a season. To make frequent inspection easy for you, place the house no higher than 5 feet from the ground. Nail or wire the house to a fencepost.

NESTING SHELVES

Essentially, a nesting shelf is a birdhouse without sides or front. American robins, phoebes, song sparrows, and barn swallows can sometimes be persuaded to use nesting shelves. Shelves should be mounted under overhanging eaves against the house, the garage, or a garden shed. In the case of American robins, a vine-covered arbor is an especially attractive location. The illustration at right shows the basic design of a nesting shelf; the dimensions given in the chart on page 72 show the size of shelf various species prefer.

A shelf for a barn swallow should be somewhat different from the shelves for other birds. The barn swallow shelf should be roofless, so it definitely needs the protection of an overhanging eave. Barn and cliff swallows nest together in communities. Both species can be encouraged to nest on the side of a building by attaching 2×4s horizontally against a wall and providing an adequate supply of mud out in the open for them to use in building nests.

BIRDHOUSE PLACEMENT

In an outdoor space of less than one acre, erecting more than one birdhouse attractive to a particular species is a waste of effort. There are a few exceptions to this rule, however. Tree swallows will accept fairly close neighbors of their own kind. Nesting boxes intended for them can be as close together as 30 feet. The boxes should be mounted on posts, well out in the open, and near water. Wrens, although territorial, like to have a considerable choice of nesting sites. The male house wren arrives early in the spring, before the female, and constructs as many as a dozen nests in his territory. He then courts a female by taking her around and showing off his work. When she finally accepts one of his nesting sites, a mating bond is formed. As often as not, the first thing she does is tear apart his hard work and start over. Because of this ritual, setting out four or more wren houses is a powerful attraction for one pair of these delightful birds.

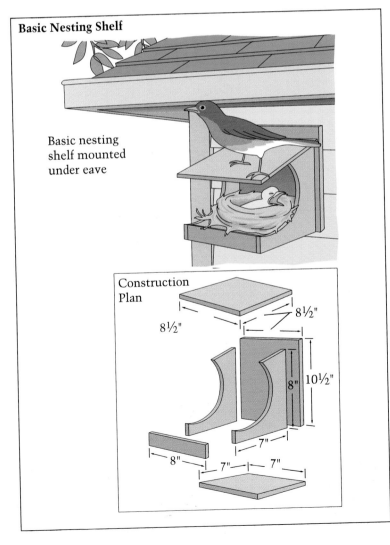

Basic Nesting Shelf

Basic nesting shelf mounted under eave

Construction Plan

8½" 8½"

8" 10½"

7"

8" 7" 7"

Dimensions for Birdhouses and Nesting Shelves

Bird	Floor of House	Height of House	Diameter of Entrance Hole	Height of Entrance Above Floor	Height Above Ground
BIRDHOUSES					
American kestrel	8"×8"	12–15"	3"	9–12"	10–30'
Eastern bluebird	5"×5"	8"	1½"	6"	5–10'
Carolina wren	4"×4"	6–8"	1½"	4–6"	6–10'
Chickadee	4"×4"	8–10"	1⅛"	6–8"	6–15'
Downy woodpecker	4"×4"	8–10"	1¼"	6–8"	6–20'
House finch	6"×6"	6"	2"	4"	8–12'
House wren	4"×4"	6–8"	1–1¼"	4–6"	6–10'
Northern flicker	7"×7"	16–18"	2½"	14–16"	6–20'
Nuthatch	4"×4"	8–10"	1¼"	6–8"	12–20'
Purple martin*	6"×6"	6"	2½"	1"	12–20'
Red-bellied woodpecker	6"×6"	12–15"	2½"	9–12"	12–20'
Red-headed woodpecker	6"×6"	12–15"	2"	9–12"	12–20'
Screech-owl	8"×8"	12–15"	3"	9–12"	10–30'
Starling	6"×6"	16–18"	2"	14–16"	10–25'
Titmouse	4"×4"	8–10"	1¼"	6–8"	6–15'
Tree swallow	5"×5"	6"	1½"	1–5"	10–15'
Winter wren	4"×4"	6–8"	1–1¼"	4–6"	6–10'
NESTING SHELVES					
American robin	6"×8"	8"			6–15'
Barn swallow	6"×6"	6"			8–12'
Phoebes	6"×6"	6"			8–12'
Song sparrow	6"×6"	6"			1–3'

*Dimensions are for one compartment (one pair of birds); martin houses are usually built eight compartments at a time. Adapted from "Homes for Birds," U.S. Department of the Interior, Fish and Wildlife Service.

Some houses built to specific dimensions for certain birds may be used by birds of a different species if they are of the same size or smaller.

Have your birdhouses up by late summer or early fall, while the leaves are still on the trees. The extent of shade, an important factor to many birds, can be determined better before the trees lose their leaves. And compared to starkly new houses, birdhouses that have aged and weathered over the winter are more attractive to birds.

If you are unable to get your birdhouses up in the early fall, plan on mounting them no later than mid-January in the mildest parts of the United States or as late as early March in the coldest. By following these guidelines, you will have a chance of attracting late-nesting birds. The northern flicker, for example, usually starts nesting around the middle of May.

BIRDHOUSE MAINTENANCE

Only a clean birdhouse will attract birds. The houses of birds that are likely to start more than one brood per season should be cleaned out as soon as the young have fledged. This is particularly important because parasites are a major cause of nestling mortality. Most birds will not use a nest a second time; they will abandon a house containing an old nest. If you clean out the box right away, they may decide to use it again; in any case, it will be ready for another pair looking for a place to raise a second brood.

To clean a house, open the removable side and remove the old nest and any debris that has collected. Dust the interior with rotenone or sulfur to destroy any parasites it might be harboring. Do this each time a pair has completed raising a brood.

PROTECTION FROM PREDATORS

Put birdhouses where cats can't reach them. Because of the threat of predators, birds are cautious about choosing a house that is on the main trunk of a tree. It's also much more difficult for you to protect tree-mounted houses from predators. Protecting a post- or a pole-mounted house from climbing intruders is much easier. If you use a wooden post, use a cone-shaped squirrel guard of the type recommended for bird feeders.

A post- or pole-mounted birdhouse is also superior because many birds prefer as a nest site an open, sunny spot rather than dense shade. Near the edge of a wood, facing south over an open expanse, is an excellent location for many birds. Open, grassy areas with a few trees—an area like an abandoned orchard—is also attractive to many. Those birds that dwell in deep woods, however—some woodpeckers, nuthatches, crested flycatchers, and chickadees—prefer forested sites.

Whether the birdhouse or shelf is placed in a tree, on a post, or under an eave or arbor, there should be a clear, unobstructed flight path to the entrance hole. Birds will use a perch from 5 to 15 feet away from the house or shelf as a point from which to survey for danger before the final approach.

*Clean out a birdhouse
after every brood.
Houses with hinged
or removable sides
are easy to care for.*

*A house wren builds a
nest in a wren box. To
attract a mating pair,
set out several wren
boxes, though the birds
will select only one.*

Attracting Your Favorite Birds

You can attract the birds you want and avoid those you don't want. This chapter summarizes ways of attracting your favorites.

Although house finches are fun to watch at the feeder and robins are delightful guests in the yard, most bird-watchers would like to attract as many different types of birds as possible. Some bird-watchers might even accept the challenge of seeing how many different kinds of birds they can identify in their own backyards. It is very exciting to record a visit from a scarlet tanager, especially if you have been trying to make your yard attractive to them.

Preceding chapters have given you a basis for attracting birds to your home; this chapter offers you specific instructions for attracting seventy of the birds most likely to visit the home landscape. The range map for each bird tells you whether that bird visits your area and at what time of year you can expect it—as a winter visitor, summer transient, or year-round resident.

The column titled "Nest Site" tells you where that bird prefers to nest. If it accepts birdhouses or nesting shelves, the entry says so; otherwise, it tells you the location it prefers for nest sites: on the ground, in trees, or in dense shrubbery.

The final column, "Behavior, Attraction Tips," tells the techniques that will be most effective for attracting that bird to your yard or garden. Some birds are most attracted to a favorite food; others, such as many insect eaters, are more easily attracted to a birdbath, nesting shelf, or specific plants.

By combining the methods described here with the information in the first chapters, you will be able to attract the widest possible variety of birds to your outdoor space.

The northern cardinal might be America's most beloved animal species—seven states have named it state bird. Among them are several northern states where the northern cardinal could not live without bird feeders.

California quail

Northern bobwhite

Bird	Range Map	Nest Site	Behavior, Attraction Tips
Northern bobwhite		Ground	An infrequent visitor to heavily planted yards near farmland. Almost always appears in coveys of up to 15 birds. The area should be free of disturbance. Usually feed on the ground. Attract by offering seeds and grain.
California quail		Ground	Well adapted to open areas in cities and residential areas. Coveys of up to several dozen birds make rounds of neighborhoods, visiting bird feeders and birdbaths. Scatter corn and mixed birdseed on the ground.
Band-tailed pigeon		Trees	Prefers open woodland with oak trees. Flocks visit heavily planted residential areas to feed on acorns, fruits, and berries. Attract by putting out sunflower seed, grain, or suet in feeders.
Mourning dove		Trees and sometimes ledges	At home almost anywhere, including urban areas. Freely visits bird feeders, sometimes in large numbers. More likely to take food on the ground than at elevated feeders. Diet limited entirely to seeds and grains.

Ruby-throated hummingbird

Red-headed woodpecker

Bird	Range Map	Nest Site	Behavior, Attraction Tips
Ruby-throated hummingbird		Trees	During migration, visits yards with lots of flowers. Sometimes stays to nest if trees are available. Prefers pink or red flowers, including beebalm, columbine, and honeysuckle. Attract by offering sugar water in feeders (see page 32).
Anna's hummingbird		Trees and odd sites	A permanent resident in many parts of the West, its range is expanding. The hummingbird most likely to reside in yards and gardens. Flowers must be present, especially those of fuchsia, coralbell, and sage.
Rufous hummingbird		Trees	Most common when passing through on migration. Drawn to yards with flowers and hummingbird feeders. Feisty males try to take over feeders. Like other hummingbirds, like to bathe in fine spray.
Red-headed woodpecker		Birdhouses and dead trees	Frequents open woodlands and yards with trees. Gathers acorns in the fall. Accepts food from platform feeders. Partial to nutmeats, cracked corn, and sunflower seed.

Eastern phoebe

Purple martin

Bird	Range Map	Nest Site	Behavior, Attraction Tips
Northern flicker		Birdhouses and dead trees	Birdhouses and open lawns are the two strongest magnets for flickers. They use lawns for foraging for ants. Less easily attracted to feeders than to ants but will eat suet, cracked corn, and nutmeats.
Black phoebe		Nesting shelves	This phoebe of the far West prefers yards where water and suitable nesting sites are available. Reasonably tolerant of disturbance.
Eastern phoebe		Nesting shelves	A place to nest is the number one requirement. When natural food is in short supply, phoebes sometimes pick up tidbits at bird feeders.
Purple martin		Martin houses (see page 69)	An open landscape with trees at a distance is essential for martins. The only food they accept is crushed eggshell on the ground below an occupied martin house.

Tree swallow

Blue jay

Bird	Range Map	Nest Site	Behavior, Attraction Tips
Tree swallow		Birdhouses that can be within 30 feet of each other	Open lawns and a place to perch (such as overhead wires) are important. Won't take food from feeding stations but will visit yards for the waxy fruits of bayberry. Sometimes substitutes small fruits for insects in fall and winter.
Violet-green swallow		Same as tree swallow	Attract by offering housing, spacious lawn, and wires for perching. Unlikely to accept fruits.
Steller's jay		Trees	Found mainly in forested mountain districts but comes into residential areas of cities. Food is the big attraction; peanuts, suet, suet mixes, and sunflower seed are the favorites.
Blue jay		Trees and shrubs	Well adapted to yards and gardens. Often nests in evergreens near houses. Noisily visits feeders, cramming its bill full of seeds and grain. Some are eaten, others stored for future use. Sunflower seed, nutmeats, and suet favored.

Scrub jay

Black-capped chickadee

Bird	Range Map	Nest Site	Behavior, Attraction Tips
Scrub jay		Trees and shrubs	Same habits as blue jay. Equally at home in wilderness or urban habitats. So long as food is offered, size of yard makes little difference.
Black-capped chickadee		Birdhouses and dead trees	Often the first bird to visit a feeding station; shows other birds the way. Frequents wooded areas, including heavily planted yards. Suet, suet mixes, sunflower seed, and nutmeats are favorite foods. Often a year-round visitor.
Mountain chickadee		Birdhouses and dead trees	Except for its mountain habitat, no different in food preferences and habits than other chickadees. Its inquisitive nature brings it to human habitations and campgrounds.
Chestnut-backed chickadee		Birdhouses and dead trees	A bird that comes freely to yards. At feeders competes with black-capped chickadee, eating the same foods.

Tufted titmouse

Red-breasted nuthatch

Bird	Range Map	Nest Site	Behavior, Attraction Tips
Plain titmouse		Birdhouses	Most at home in oak and pinyon-juniper woodlands but readily comes into residential areas. Attract by offering food at feeders. As might be expected of a member of the chickadee family, fond of sunflower seed, suet, and doughnuts.
Tufted titmouse		Birdhouses	In the East, takes the place of the plain titmouse. Prefers yards with trees; able to master almost any feeder. Favors nutmeats, suet, and sunflower seed.
Bushtit		Trees and shrubs	Tiny birds that travel in flocks. Attracted to heavily planted yards. Mostly eats insects, but may sample suet, suet mixes, and peanut butter. Swarms over feeders and quickly leaves.
Red-breasted nuthatch		Birdhouses	Usually seen only in winter, in populated regions. Feeds largely on pine seeds but attracted to feeders containing suet, suet mixes, sunflower seed, and nutmeats.

White-breasted nuthatch

Carolina wren

Bird	Range Map	Nest Site	Behavior, Attraction Tips
White-breasted nuthatch		Birdhouses	More of a nuteater than the red-breasted nuthatch. Prefers woodlands and yards having oaks and other deciduous trees. A year-round visitor to bird feeders, never seeming to tire of suet, sunflower seed, and nutmeats.
Brown creeper		Under loose bark, but will accept "artificial" sites	So long as trees are present, winter visits by this tree-loving bird are possible. Too timid to come to feeders when other birds are present, but will sample suet mixes smeared on bark.
Cactus wren		Cactus or a thorny shrub	A desert bird that has moved into heavily planted residential areas. Freely patronizes bird feeders, eating a wide variety of foods. Prefers suet, nutmeats, and watermelon.
Carolina wren		Birdhouses, nooks, hanging baskets	Very bold about coming to bird feeders of all kinds. Offer food near shrubbery or brush piles. Prefers suet, suet mixes, bakery products, and nutmeats.

Eastern bluebird

Western bluebird

Bird	Range Map	Nest Site	Behavior, Attraction Tips
House wren		Birdhouses and nooks	Prefers yards with tangles and woodpiles. Housing is the primary attraction. Rarely takes anything at the feeder.
Golden-crowned kinglet		Trees (mostly evergreens)	A winter visitor that prefers yards with conifers. Often seen fluttering around needles, in search of insects or insect eggs. Occasionally samples suet, suet mixes, or peanut butter.
Ruby-crowned Kinglet		Trees	Habits similar to those of the golden-crowned kinglet, but more likely to appear in yards in winter and visit feeders. Offer suet, suet mixes, and nutmeats.
Eastern Bluebird		Birdhouses (see page 70)	Properly placed nesting boxes are best attraction. Seldom appears in yards in urban areas. Food in plain view, especially in winter, can draw the bluebird to feeders. Will eat suet, bakery products, raisins, and berries.
Western bluebird		Birdhouses	Like its eastern cousin, this bluebird responds well to housing and berry-bearing ornamentals. Occasionally visits feeders and birdbaths.

Hermit thrush

American robin

Bird	Range Map	Nest Site	Behavior, Attraction Tips
Hermit thrush		Trees	In the winter, a heavily planted yard can serve as substitute habitat for this bird of wild habitats. Freely visits feeders and birdbaths. Prefers steamed raisins, nutmeats, suet, and some seeds.
American robin		Trees and nesting shelves	Favors lawns for finding worms and fruit and berry-bearing trees and shrubs. Usually comes to feeders only in bad weather. Prefers bread, softened raisins, and suet. Uses birdbaths for drinking and bathing.
Varied thrush		Trees	In fall and winter, this reclusive bird of forested mountain slopes appears in the lowlands. Attract by offering fruits, berries, and water. Halved apples and, sometimes, bakery products can bring it to feeding stations.
Wrentit		Shrubs	A seldom-seen bird of coastal thickets. Sugar-water feeders might bring it out into the open. Will also sample suet, peanut butter, and bread.
Gray catbird		Shrubs	Generally keeps to dense shrubbery but will come out onto lawns. Prefers soft foods such as steamed raisins and cooked breakfast cereal, but will eat seeds and grains that have been softened by moisture. One of the most frequent visitors to birdbaths.

Brown thrasher

Cedar waxwing

Bird	Range Map	Nest Site	Behavior, Attraction Tips
Northern mockingbird		Shrubs	Frequently stays out in the open. Vigorously defends its territory against other birds. This can mean defending berry-bearing plants and even bird feeders. Fond of softened raisins, doughnuts, sliced apples, and oranges.
Brown thrasher		Shrubs	A ground-loving bird that keeps to shrubbery, but might dash into the open to get food at feeders. Prefers seeds, grains, nutmeats, bakery products, and halved oranges. Offer food on or near the ground.
Curve-billed thrasher		Cactus (usually)	Has moved into residential areas. Does well amid irrigated greenery. Patronizes both bird feeders and birdbaths. Tastes run to cracked corn, milo, millet, and sliced watermelon.
Cedar waxwing		Trees and shrubs	Fruits and berries—including those of mountain ash, mulberry, cherry, and crab apple—are the dietary mainstays of this waxwing and also of the Bohemian waxwing. Can also be lured to water, halved apples, or steamed raisins.
Orange-crowned warbler		On or near the ground	The orange-crowned warbler is a winter visitor to feeders almost anywhere throughout its wide range. Offer suet, suet mixes, peanut butter, and chopped nutmeats.

Scarlet tanager

Western tanager

Bird	Range Map	Nest Site	Behavior, Attraction Tips
Yellow warbler		Trees and shrubs	One of the few warblers that nests in residential areas. Prefers heavily planted yards with some parts left as tangles. Water, especially in motion, attracts this bright yellow bird.
Yellow-rumped warbler		Trees	The most likely warbler in yards and at feeding stations. Very common during migration, less so in winter. Fond of suet, suet mixes, peanut butter, and bakery products. Feeds on fruits of bayberry in the wild.
Summer tanager		Trees	A lucky day indeed to have a visit from a tanager! None of the four species that nest within our borders are common. They may visit feeders for fresh fruit, raisins, suet, and nutmeats—especially in the winter.
Scarlet tanager		Trees	If, by good luck, you have a nesting pair, offer fruit on platform feeders. Also offer sugar water.
Western tanager		Trees	Use the same tactics for the western tanager as for the others. It requires luck to get it to a feeder, but once it discovers a food supply, the winter stray becomes a steady visitor.

Northern cardinal

Indigo bunting

Bird	Range Map	Nest Site	Behavior, Attraction Tips
Northern cardinal		Trees and shrubs	Prefers trees and shrubs, especially those that produce seed or fruit crops. Offer sunflower seed, nutmeats, suet, melon seeds, and bakery products. Food should be easily accessible. Prefers food on or close to the ground.
Rose-breasted grosbeak		Trees and shrubs	To increase the chance of having this colorful, appealing bird at your bird feeder, continue to offer food in summer. Food and water may induce it to stay. Offer sunflower seed, mixed birdseed, suet, and melon seeds.
Lazuli bunting		Shrubs and vines	Only during migration is this brightly colored bunting likely to stop off for a few days and join other birds at bird feeders. Prefers mixed bird-seed containing millet.
Indigo bunting		Shrubs and saplings	The common bunting in the East. Unlikely to stop in a home landscape except during migration. Besides millet, offer canary seed and finely chopped nutmeats.
Rufous-sided towhee		Ground (usually)	These normally timid birds will leave the shrub-bery for food on the ground. Prefers sunflower seed, mixed birdseed, nutmeats, and bakery products when few other birds are feeding.

Fox sparrow

Song sparrow

Bird	Range Map	Nest Site	Behavior, Attraction Tips
California and canyon towhees		Trees and shrubs	Easily attracted to yards containing birdbaths and feeding stations at ground level. Will accept almost any seeds and grains, but prefers sunflower seed, cracked corn, and millet.
American tree sparrow		On or near the ground	Bad-weather birds, they flock to feeders when the snow falls, then wander far afield when the storm is over. Will take suet, sunflower seed, and mixed birdseed from platform and hanging feeders.
Chipping sparrow		Trees and shrubs	Prefers open yards with scattered trees and shrubs. In summer or winter it comes to food scattered on the ground. Bread crumbs, mixed birdseed, and almost anything that falls from hanging feeders are to its liking.
Fox sparrow		On or near the ground	Feeds on the ground, energetically scratching to turn up whatever it can find. Never venturing far from cover, goes over and over the same ground near and below bird feeders. Favors mixed birdseed, bits of suet, and nutmeats.
Song sparrow		On or near the ground	Prefers yards that are not overly trimmed and tidy. Offer sunflower seed, niger seed, mixed birdseed, and bread. A frequent visitor to birdbaths.

Dark-eyed junco

White-crowned sparrow

Bird	Range Map	Nest Site	Behavior, Attraction Tips
White-throated sparrow		On or near the ground	Prefers wooded yards with ample cover. Does nearly all feeding on the ground, where it sees that none of the fallen sunflower or niger seed is wasted. Mixed birdseed is the only food it really needs.
Golden-crowned sparrow		On or near the ground	The Far West is treated to the appearance in the fall of both golden- and white-crowned sparrows. Besides eating the usual sparrow foods, golden-crowned birds pluck buds and blossoms from some garden plants.
White-crowned sparrow		On or near the ground	This far-ranging bird is regarded as the most handsome of the sparrows native to North America. Offer food on the ground and water in the birdbaths. Eats the usual sparrow foods as well as rapeseed, buckwheat, and apples.
Dark-eyed junco		The ground (usually)	Aptly called snow birds, juncos often arrive at feeders with the first snowfall. Flicking their tails, they feed on the ground or the snow. Offer seeds, nutmeats, and bakery products.
Orchard oriole		Trees	Attracted by fruit, which lures it to bird feeders. The best way to bring these retiring orioles down from the trees is to offer sugar water in nectar feeders. Usually present only during the summer nesting season.

Northern oriole

Purple finch

Bird	Range Map	Nest Site	Behavior, Attraction Tips
Hooded oriole		Trees	Easy to attract if you have the right trees for nesting (palms, in warmer sections), flowers that offer nectar, and nectar feeders for orioles. Fruit and halved watermelon are on its menu.
Northern oriole		Trees	It places its pendant nest in shade trees and eagerly accepts food from bird feeders. Accepts most foods, including millet, suet, softened raisins, and halved apples and oranges. Also takes sugar water from hummingbird or oriole feeders.
Purple finch		Trees (usually conifers)	Large numbers of northern finches, including this one, invade the South only some years. Offer a plentiful supply of sunflower seed. Hearty eaters, they will also sample mixed birdseed, niger seed, and nutmeats. They prefer elevated feeders.
House finch		Trees, shrubs, vines, and hanging baskets	Common in the West and overrunning the East since its introduction in 1941, the house finch is now one of the most common visitors to bird feeders. Offer plenty of seeds, especially sunflower and niger. Also offer water.

Evening grosbeak

American goldfinch

Bird	Range Map	Nest Site	Behavior, Attraction Tips
Common redpoll		Low down in trees	You have to wait for "invasion" years to catch sight of this far northern finch. When flocks do arrive, they fearlessly come to food on the ground or in feeders. Offer nutmeats, suet, and sunflower and niger seeds.
Pine siskin		Trees	Nomadic wanderers, pine siskins, like other northern finches, come southward some years and not others. Flocks inundate feeders and cover the ground. Offer suet, sunflower and niger seeds, and mixed birdseed.
American goldfinch		Trees and shrubs	These colorful finches will come to mature heads of garden flowers to collect the harvest. Offer niger and sunflower seeds and mixed birdseed. Water, especially water in motion, is one of the surest lures of all.
Evening grosbeak		Trees	Food is the key to having these spectacular guests from the north. Offer fruits from trees or sunflower seed at feeders. Appearances in the southern part of the range have been less frequent in recent years.

As Your Interest Grows

You couldn't ask for a safer and more benevolent hobby than attracting birds. About the only "danger" with this pursuit is its addictive nature. As you become more interested in your visitors, you will want to learn more about them. To help you with this, some basic equipment will be useful.

A pair of binoculars kept handy at your favorite viewing window will bring the images of shy visitors, the ones that hang around the fringes of your garden, up close for better observation.

A field guide is essential to the positive identification of a species, and many excellent ones are available. A good field guide is pocket-sized and lightweight, strongly bound to withstand frequent use, and has a stain- and water-resistant cover. Illustrations should be in full color and show distinguishing traits. Clear, concise descriptions are necessary for identifying a species in its various forms: a male in breeding and nonbreeding plumage, a female, a juvenile, and geographical variations. The guide should be organized by bird families, not by habitats or plumage coloration. Before you buy a field guide, read the introduction to be sure that it complies with the most recent authority for nomenclature, the American Ornithologists' Union Check-list of North American Birds, sixth edition. The nomenclature of older books is based on the fifth edition, published in 1957, which is considerably different and obsolete.

Keeping Track of Your Visitors
Well-kept records can greatly increase your enjoyment of your bird-attracting program. Records reveal what you are doing right and should continue, as well as unsuccessful approaches that are unnecessary or wasteful. Keeping notes also focuses your attention and gives your observations structure. If you want to get really involved, your notes can even provide valuable information that organizations for bird research may welcome.

With a notebook, pen, binoculars, and field guide next to your favorite viewing window, you're all set. Each time you make an observation, note the date, the time of day, and what the weather is like. Stagger your observation periods to compile information about the schedules of birds. The list that follows presents aspects of bird behavior to observe to create a fascinating profile of your visitors.

1. Feeding habits, including how birds find, open, and eat their food and if some of the food is stored or buried for future use

2. Foods eaten at the feeding station. (For discussion of testing tray experiments, see page 37.)

3. How birds vie for position at feeders—which individuals and species are dominant and which must wait their turn

4. Arrival and departure dates

5. Numbers and species visiting the bird feeders and birdbaths

6. Bathing and drinking habits

7. Careful descriptions (preferably drawings or photographs) of rare or unexpected guests and "mystery birds" that you are unable to identify

8. Careful descriptions of and notes about birds that exhibit strange coloring or unfamiliar plumage

9. Birds that have physical disabilities, such as only one leg

10. Birdcalls, such as alarm notes, and how other birds react to them

11. Bird injuries and mortality, including losses from window strikes, predation, and disease

12. Nesting, including location and type of nest, nesting materials used, date nest completed, number of eggs laid, number that hatched, and number of young leaving the nest and when

Joining With Others
There are many ways to share your interest in birds with others. Several magazines focus on watching and attracting birds. You can join clubs at either the local or national level. You can even help with backyard research projects.

One of the best ways to expand your activity is by joining the National Wildlife Federation and participating in its Backyard Wildlife Program. This program is designed for people with property from windowsill size to up to 3 acres. Applicants who agree to provide certain minimum requirements of food, water, and shelter receive a Backyard Wildlife Registration Certificate in addition to a newsletter and a large list of publications that can be ordered. For further information write to the federation at the address that follows.

Backyard Wildlife Program, National Wildlife Federation, 1412 Sixteenth Street NW, Washington, DC 20036

If you would like to contribute to knowledge about birds that visit feeders, join Project FeederWatch. This continent-wide survey is sponsored by the Cornell Laboratory of Ornithology. The laboratory, with help from thousands of participants, studies feeder-bird populations and other feeder-related subjects. Participants support the survey with a subscription to the bi-annual newsletter, which contains up-to-date results and much more.

Project FeederWatch, Cornell Laboratory of Ornithology, 159 Sapsucker Woods Road, Ithaca, NY 14850

A subscription to any of the following publications, newsletters, and magazines will keep you informed regarding techniques of bird-attracting and the experiences of other people in this field.

American Birds, 700 Broadway, New York, NY 10003 (published by the National Audubon Society)

Bird Watcher's Digest, Box 110, Marietta, OH 45750

Birder's World, 720 East Eighth Street, Holland, MI 49423

The Bird's Eye reView, National Bird-Feeding Society, Box 23, Northbrook, IL 60065-0023

Living Bird Quarterly, Cornell Laboratory of Ornithology, 159 Sapsucker Woods Road, Ithaca, NY 14850

Nature Society News, Griggsville, IL 62340

Wildbird, Box 6050, Mission Viejo, CA 92690

Before you know it, you may find yourself stalking the wilds beyond your property lines, searching for the bird that just won't come into the yard. Birdwatching, listing, and photography are popular activities, and many local clubs and societies, too numerous to list here, sponsor field trips and informative programs. The first place to check is your local chapter of the National Audubon Society. If you have difficulty finding a chapter near you, write to the national headquarters of the organization.

National Audubon Society, 700 Broadway, New York, NY 10003

INDEX

Note: Page numbers in boldface type indicate principal references; page numbers in italic type indicate references to illustrations.

U.S. Measure and Metric Measure Conversion Chart

Formulas for Exact Measures

	Symbol	When you know:	Multiply by:	To find:
Mass (weight)	oz	ounces	28.35	grams
	lb	pounds	0.45	kilograms
	g	grams	0.035	ounces
	kg	kilograms	2.2	pounds
Volume	pt	pints	0.47	liters
	qt	quarts	0.95	liters
	gal	gallons	3.785	liters
	ml	milliliters	0.034	fluid ounces
Length	in.	inches	2.54	centimeters
	ft	feet	30.48	centimeters
	yd	yards	0.9144	meters
	mi	miles	1.609	kilometers
	km	kilometers	0.621	miles
	m	meters	1.094	yards
	cm	centimeters	0.39	inches
Temperature	°F	Fahrenheit	$\frac{5}{9}$ (after subtracting 32)	Celsius
	°C	Celsius	$\frac{9}{5}$ (then add 32)	Fahrenheit
Area	in.^{2}	square inches	6.452	square centimeters
	ft^2	square feet	929.0	square centimeters
	yd^2	square yards	8361.0	square centimeters
	a.	acres	0.4047	hectares

Rounded Measures for Quick Reference

1 oz		= 30 g
4 oz		= 115 g
8 oz		= 225 g
16 oz	= 1 lb	= 450 g
32 oz	= 2 lb	= 900 g
36 oz	= 2¼ lb	= 1000 g (1 kg)
1 c	= 8 oz	= 250 ml
2 c (1 pt)	= 16 oz	= 500 ml
4 c (1 qt)	= 32 oz	= 1 liter
4 qt (1 gal)	= 128 oz	= 3¾ liter
⅜ in.	= 1.0 cm	
1 in.	= 2.5 cm	
2 in.	= 5.0 cm	
2½ in.	= 6.5 cm	
12 in. (1 ft)	= 30 cm	
1 yd	= 90 cm	
100 ft	= 30 m	
1 mi	= 1.6 km	
32° F	= 0° C	
212° F	= 100° C	
1 in.^{2}	= 6.5 cm^2	
1 ft^2	= 930 cm^2	
1 yd^2	= 8360 cm^2	
1 a.	= 4050 m^2	